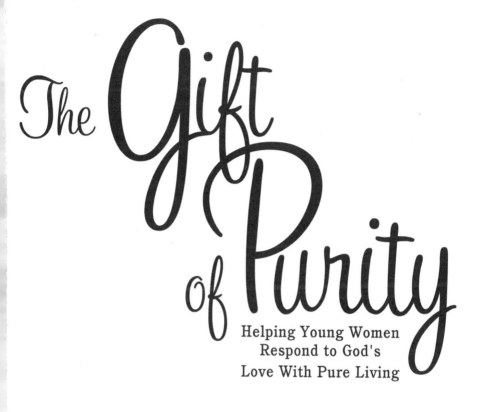

The Gift of Purity

Helping Young Women Respond to God's Love With Pure Living

RACHEL WELBORN

GOSPEL ADVOCATE

A TRUSTED NAME SINCE 1855

Published by Gospel Advocate Co.
1006 Elm Hill Pike, Nashville, TN 37210
www.gospeladvocate.com

ISBN: 978-0-89225-596-2

Dedication

When I begin to think of all the many people who have had a hand in shaping the words of this book in some way, the list is immense. Encouragers in my professional career, church family, and physical family have lined my path to this point. I see the faces of the many young women who have walked through this material with me as I sought to design its content. You are all precious to me. And Bethany, your insights and encouragement kept me motivated to move forward.

At the finish line, though, stands my greatest supporter and cheerleader, my sweet husband, Jerry, who washed dishes, did shopping, and drove the car so I could write on long trips – and anything else I needed so this book could take shape. Thank you, Love. As the children have taught us to say, "I love you more."

Above all, praise be to God, who blesses us with His guidance and love. He is the reason for this book as He is the loving Giver of our gift of purity.

Table of Contents

Foreword

For more than 20 years, I have been teaching young women in Bible classes at Freed-Hardeman University. In those classes, we discuss the roles a woman has in her physical family and in her spiritual family. We examine how we can reflect our heavenly Father to the world around us and how we are to be holy because He is holy (1 Peter 1:15-16). During those years, I have searched for material on purity that would be both biblically and factually accurate and that would discuss purity as a way of life rather than a checklist of things Christians should or should not do. In this book, I found that balance.

You are living in a world that tells you there is no absolute truth. It wants you to believe that sin is no longer sin; it is a choice. You are encouraged to do what feels good to you in the moment. The world does not tell you what results from that type of life, and knowing those results is very relevant as you make significant decisions at this time in your life. Rachel Welborn asks some of the hard questions you are dealing with right now as you try to live a godly life. She also gives you accurate information that will help you answer those hard questions.

In this book you will find a wealth of information about subjects such as hormones; sexual foreplay; sexually transmitted infections; and the physical, mental and emotional consequences of an impure lifestyle. You will study some of the God-given differences between males and females. Yet underlying all of this is the concept that "we have a God who loves us completely, who always functions from a position of truth, and who has our long-term best interest at heart. So when He guides us, we can stand confidently in the knowledge that where He is leading will always be the best path for us in every way."

The book is designed to allow you to explore and reflect on specific biblical passages. Through guided discussion and activities in class, the meaning of those passages and their application to your life should become clearer. You will learn that real purity is living in such a way that your heart, soul, mind and strength are focused on God. After studying this book, you will be armed with the knowledge that will allow you to make informed choices so that you might live an abundant life (John 10:10) with fewer regrets.

– DWINA WILLIS
HENDERSON, TENN.

About the Author

My Experience

From my earliest professional career choice, I have been passionate about helping young people get off to a good start in life. That passion initially led me to the classroom as a teacher of first grade and ninth grade students, which provided a wide range of experience with youth on a day-to-day basis. It was my work with young teenage moms, though, that began to provide a focus for the passion I felt.

As a parent educator working with the local school district, my responsibility was to visit one-on-one with young moms and their babies at least once a month to provide guidance on a range of issues. Listening to these young women's stories and watching them struggle with the burdens of caring for a young life alone weighed heavily upon my heart. While all of these mothers loved their babies dearly, none of them wanted to face the challenge of being a single parent. Many times I thought, "If I could have only talked to them sooner …"

A few short years later, God placed in my hands the opportunity to do just that – talk to young teens before they became sexually active.

As a youth health educator, my entire job description was to design and deliver abstinence education to junior high students across an entire school district. What a tremendous opportunity and challenge! Training older teens to lead sessions with the younger teens provided insights into reaching both age groups.

After three years, I became the "front and center" presenter in classrooms set in a rural school district. Concern for teens in the district led the superintendent and principals to welcome me into the fifth through seventh grade classrooms for an opportunity to share with the youth the value of saving sex until marriage.

These two professional opportunities provided experience and training to help me become comfortable and knowledgeable as a presenter on this challenging subject. In a short time, I began to get requests from the church community, speaking at summer youth camps, girls' retreats, regularly scheduled teen and college-age Bible classes, and mother/daughter events. During the course of 10 years of constantly building and refining the material I presented, I began to get requests to put the lessons in writing. This book is a product of those requests.

My Family and Interests

Almost 30 years ago, I married my best friend, Jerry. Much of that 30-year experience has been within the context of full-time ministry throughout the South. Together, we have had the joy of watching our two sons, Bryan and Andrew, grow to maturity and begin families of their own. Bryan married Bethany Wagar, the author of "Insights From Bethany" included in this book. Andrew recently expanded our family circle by marrying Leah Ballard. God continues to bless us through our children and through our ever-expanding church family.

More to the Story

Why another book on sexual purity? For me, the answer is simple: because there is more to the story. So much of modern abstinence material focuses on only one or two aspects of sexual purity. For instance, many have written about health risks, which are very real concerns that certainly are not to be ignored. Other great books have been written about the damage that sexual impurity causes in later relationships – another imperative topic.

Yet above all of this is the overarching message that I think sometimes fails to get the attention it deserves: that is, the story of our incredible Maker who seeks to shield His little children from a colossal realm of pain. When He directs – yes, commands – He does so out of love. He, above all others, knows how He fashioned us. He knows what will cause us pain and brokenness, and He seeks to shield us through His Word. This book is an exploration of His love and how He displays an awesome wisdom and compassion as He guides us through life's difficult choices. This is a love story, and we are the receivers of the love.

How to Use This Book

Read About It

First and foremost, this book is intended to be a Bible study complement, not a replacement for Bible study on this important topic. So when you reach sections labeled "Read About It," stop, open God's Word, and dig in.

Think About It

Once you have your Bible open and are exploring the direction provided, take the time to meditate on what the words mean to your life. The "Think About It" sections are designed to help you apply the scriptures to the topic being discussed. Use this time to write your reflections. You may choose to write them in this book or in a journal. Whichever method you choose, I recommend you keep your thoughts in one place so you can reflect back on them as you move through the interlaced lessons.

Pray About It

At the close of each lesson is a section titled "Pray About It." These sections are not intended to become rote prayers offered by individuals or groups. Instead, these are simply thoughts to consider as you form your own conversation with our Father. Our loving God who created us relishes time spent with His daughters. Talk to Him. He welcomes you.

This book can be used to guide individual study or group study. However, this is one topic where having like-minded friends to provide encouragement is extremely important. So even if you are choosing to read this book on your own, you might consider inviting a friend to read it also so you can strengthen and encourage each other. I also encourage you to join the discussion at **www.facebook.com/GiftOfPurity**. This is a great place to post any comments, insights or questions you might have along the way.

About "Insights From Bethany"

As I was working to put these thoughts in writing, I was very honored to have had Bethany Wagar, a then 19-year-old sophomore at Freed-Hardeman University, reading over my shoulder. Bethany has provided invaluable insights and suggestions, some of which were directly incorporated and some which stand alone in her own words. I chose Bethany because of her high integrity and godliness. After the first draft of this book was submitted to the publisher, my son Bryan chose Bethany as his wife. He chose well!

Chapter 1

God Is

Opening Reflections

Living in Mississippi means being well-acquainted with hurricanes. So as Hurricane Katrina was about to make landfall in 2005, we, along with thousands of others in our state, began to make our usual preparations. But no one was prepared for the catastrophe that we experienced over the days that followed. Entire blocks, neighborhoods, antebellum homes and other monuments were completely swept away. Pictures do not begin to capture the breadth of the devastation.

A few weeks later, while we were still reeling from the storm, we had a guest from Jamaica visit our home. Katrina being a common topic, I asked him how often they had to rebuild his community because of tropical storm and hurricane damage. His answer surprised me.

"Never."

"Why is that so?" I asked. His simple answer floored me!

"Because we build our structures to withstand the storms."

He then went on to describe how the foundations were laid and how the walls were anchored securely so that their homes would withstand these devastating winds. Granted, the concrete block walls reinforced with rebar securely fastened to thick foundations might not make the cover of a popular home and garden magazine, but in the end lives are saved, and homes are secure.

As we travel down to the hardest hit coastal areas years out from Katrina and view the still desolate regions, I've often wondered what it would have been like if the foundations had been solid and the walls securely anchored.

Starting Point

How would you complete this sentence: "God is _____"?

You may be thinking this is an odd place to start a book on nurturing and protecting who we are as God's daughters. I hope that by the end of this lesson it will make sense. You see, without a strong foundation, you simply can't build a strong building – one that will last through the storms ahead. The same is true for building strong relationships. You need to get the foundation in place before trying to build anything lasting on top of it.

Going back to the opening thought, you could have picked all kinds of words to describe who God is. Maybe you chose a word that describes His power, such as awesome, mighty or omnipotent (which means all-powerful). Or maybe you chose a word that describes His heart, such as loving, tender, compassionate or forgiving. You could have described His holiness with words like pure, righteous or just. Or perhaps you chose a word that describes one of His roles, such as Father, Creator or Judge. Although any of these, and a host of other words, accurately depict some part of who God is, one particular "God is" phrase found in the Bible is significant to this exploration.

 Read About It

1 John 4:7-17

How did John complete this sentence: "God is _____" (see vv. 8, 16)?

God is love. This is one of many ways that the Bible tells us who God is. Notice something important though. John didn't just say, "God loves us." Although, of course, He does. And he didn't just say, "God is loving," which, of course, is also true. What he did say, though, goes even deeper. God *is* love!

Think back to grade school English class. When you use the word "is" in a sentence with a noun on each side of it, what does that mean? It means the two nouns are the same, right? For instance, "Susan is a girl" means the same as "Susan equals girl." The two are the same. This person is Susan, and this person is a girl.

"Okay," you may be thinking, "why is this so important?"

Think about it a minute. Suppose I said to you, "Susan plays basketball." What would that mean? You might say simply that she likes the game or maybe even that she is good at it. But suppose I said: "Wow! Susan *is* basketball!" You'd probably get a different idea.

Just the fact that we don't often put words together like that would probably get your attention. But you would probably also get the idea that basketball is so much a part of Susan's life that she has just *become* a part of the game itself. Do you hear the passion? She is completely immersed in the sport. She is the same as basketball. She *is* basketball!

Well, God *is* love. Love is so much a part of who He is that it *is* who He is. There is no part of Him that is not love. God equals love. And whom does He love? This all-love God chooses to love you and me.

Think About It

• How does it make you feel to think about God being all love?

• How does it make you feel to know that He is giving all of that love to you?

Depending on where you are in your life, you may have very different feelings about God's love for you. For example, you may think of God's love as a very wonderful place to rest, sort of like having a warm place to snuggle on a cold winter day. Or maybe it's a little harder for you to find comfort in God's love. Maybe you struggle with not feeling worthy or somehow not measuring up. Or maybe you see God as more of the lightning-bolt-from-the-sky-when-I-mess-up kind of God.

Regardless of where you are, though, we are assured of God's love for us. So much comfort and assurance are found in what Romans 5:8 says: "But God demonstrates His own love toward us, in that while we were yet sinners, Christ died for us." God didn't sit around waiting for us to "deserve" His love before He offered His love. Notice that He did all of this "while we were yet sinners." Does that mean He is always happy with our choices? Of course not. But it does mean that He *always* loves. God is love.

Now, back to how this fits together in our study on purity. If God loves – in fact *is* love – then whatever He desires for us will always be out of pure love for us. He will never desire things just to be cruel or to take our fun away because that is not the way true love acts. So if God says something about how to live our lives, He is saying it out of love. He created us out of love. If He places a limit on our lives, He is placing the limit out of love. All that He does or says is guided by love.

Think about it this way: We all have people we love, and because of that love, we try to do what is right toward them all the time. But we are human, and that means we mess up – a lot! We slip up and do or say hurtful things – sometimes out of anger, selfishness or just weariness. God, however, is God. He always loves, all the time – and perfectly. So He does not make mistakes in demonstrating His love.

Think About It
• What are some examples of God's love that you see in your life?

• Name some people you know who are good examples of the unselfish love that God offers. How do you see them demonstrating this love?

Let's look at another "God is" statement.

Read About It
1 John 1:5-7

How was this sentence completed in verse 5: "God is _____"?

Think About It
What do light and darkness represent in these verses?

Add to the picture, then, that God is light. We know from nature that light and dark are opposites. In these verses, the same is true. Because God is light, there can be no darkness in Him at all (v. 5). If a room is *completely* filled with light, there cannot be even a shadow in the room. Likewise, if a room is *completely* dark, it is all the way dark. That means no night lights, no flicker of light under the door – nothing. The end of 1 John 1 illustrates that light and dark can be compared to righteousness and sin. John also pointed this out in another passage.

Read About It

John 3:19-21

Think About It

- Who is the light in this passage (see vv. 16-18)?

- Where do you see examples in your life of this difference between darkness and light?

Jesus is the light here. Those who do evil (darkness) hate the light. Those who love the truth come to the light (v. 21). So clearly, evil and darkness go together while light and truth go together.

Think About It

- If we know God is light (truth), what can we learn about how He guides us?

- Have you ever been in a completely dark place? How did it feel to move around without being able to see anything? How did you feel once you got to a place where you had light? How does this experience relate to our walk with God in His light?

- Has there ever been a time in your life when God's truth "lit the path" to a right decision for you? If so, how did it feel to have His guidance?

Knowing God is light (truth), we can step forward in full confidence onto the path that He shows us. We don't have to fear what is lurking in the dark as long as we walk on God's well-lit path.

Recap

We know, first, that God is love all the time, all the way. So what He does or says is always guided by His love for us. Second, we know God is also light. That means everything He does is always true and right. He will never lie to us or try to lead us down a path that isn't right. He will always guide us to truth (light) out of love for us. Now, consider one more "God is" statement to finish the foundation.

Read About It
John 4:24

How was this sentence completed in this verse: "God is _____"?
This one was easy to find – right there in the first three words. But even though the word may have been easy to find, this is a tough idea to grasp. We – human, fleshly beings that we are – get very caught up in the tangibles of life; that is, what we can see, hear, touch, taste and feel. But God is not fleshly and physical like us; He is a spirit. And we, having been created in His image, have a spirit too – our souls.

The unique thing about God as a spirit and about our souls is that the two will continue on after the fleshly part of our bodies has crumbled in the ground. Why does that matter? God, as spirit, created us to also have a spirit (soul) that will carry on throughout eternity. It is the part of us that matters the most because it will last long after this human body is gone.

Here is how this fits: We all recognize that sometimes taking care of someone means doing what matters the most in the long run. For instance, when you were little, you may have asked your mom for a candy bar for breakfast. Chances are she said no. But why? It would have made you happy. Why would she say no to something that would make you happy? You know the answer: She was more interested in what would be best for you in the long run than what might make you happy for a minute.

That makes sense because that's how true love acts. So if God – who is all love – tells you something, first of all, you know it will be guided by **love**. Second, you know it will be true (**light**). And third, you can know it will be guided by what is best for you in the long run (**spirit**), not by what might make you happy for a moment.

Think About It

- Think about a time when someone who loves you told you no because it was best for you in the long run. How did you feel about it in the moment? How did you feel about it after you realized it was for your good?

- How does it make you feel to think about God guiding you from the love, light and spirit perspectives?

Summing It Up

We have a God who **loves** us completely, who always functions from a position of truth **(light)**, and who has our long-term best interest at heart **(spirit)**. So when He guides us, we can stand confidently in the knowledge that where He is leading will always be the best path for us in every way. We may not always understand everything that He says. It may not make sense to us or be what everyone else is doing. But if our love-light-spirit God tells us something, we can be sure it is the right and best path for our lives.

Talk About It

1. How does thinking about these characteristics of God influence the way you view His commands?

2. Where do you see God's love, light and spirit reflected in the verse below?

   "For God so loved the world, that He gave His only begotten Son, that whoever believes in Him shall not perish, but have eternal life" (John 3:16).

3. How can you demonstrate trust in God's love, light and spirit on a daily basis?

Pray About It

Dear Lord, we are so grateful that You are love, light and spirit. We pray that You will help us take hold of Your direction with complete confidence, knowing You will always guide us in the way that is best, right and guided by an immeasurable love for us. Thank You, Father.

Chapter 2

Fearfully and Wonderfully Made

Recap

From the previous lesson, we learned three important traits about God. God is love, light and spirit. Because of these three elements, we can be assured that whatever He says or does for our lives is completely out of a loving heart (**love**), is absolutely true (**light**), and always has our long-term best interest in mind (**spirit**). In this lesson, we will explore three truths about ourselves and how this loving God created and interacts with us.

Opening Reflections

Growing up, the teen years were tough for me. I wore glasses (and not the cute ones of today), was short, and was a little "thick" in places. My attempts at getting a golden tan resulted in millions of freckles. And my crooked teeth led to infrequent smiling. Add to that the fact that I was one of only a handful of Christian teens in my very large high school graduating class. I often thought of myself as ugly, unpopular and alone.

Then, I met a young woman just a few years older than me. Like me, she was not likely to make the cover of any of the latest glamour magazines, yet everyone flocked to her. Frankly, I was a little perplexed by her popularity. It defied everything I had seen of what being attractive meant. However, as I grew to know her better, I understood. She was (and still is) one of the most beautiful people I know. You see, her beauty from within is so overwhelming that nothing at the surface has a chance of overshadowing her true radiance. This dear friend, more than anyone else in my life, has taught me what it means to be beautiful.

Starting Point

When you look at your image in the mirror, what do you see? What do you like about what you see? What do you not like?

If you are like most women, these questions make you uncomfortable. It absolutely amazes me how many women don't like their images in the mirror. We are quick to see the little blemishes, bulges or a host of other little details that to us keep us from measuring up to the "perfect" image.

Suppose for a minute that this picture was different. What if, when you looked into the mirror, the image you saw was truly beautiful and lovely in every way that you can imagine? What if you were totally satisfied with the image you saw? What would that be like?

Now, we know that an image is not exactly the same as the person or thing it is representing, but it is very close to what is real. So what if I told you that your image *is* beautiful and lovely?

Read About It

- Genesis 1:26-27
- Psalm 27:4

Truth #1: We are created in the image of our beautiful God.

Think About It

- In what ways is God beautiful?

- If God is beautiful and we are created in His image, then what does that say about us?

- What do you think it means to be created in God's image?

- How can we reflect His beauty?

- Think of five women who you really think reflect God's beauty. What is attractive about them? In what ways do you want to be like them?

- Now, think of five women who the world sees as beautiful or "hot." Why does the world call them beautiful? How does the worldly image of beauty compare to the beauty of God?

Let's read on to discover the second truth of this study.

Read About It
Psalm 139:13-16

Truth #2: We are fearfully and wonderfully made.

Think About It
What do you think about the phrase "fearfully and wonderfully made"?

You may find the idea of being "wonderfully made" appealing, but maybe you aren't so sure about the "fearfully made" part. Let's dig into these two words to get a better picture of what God is telling us.

You may already know that the Old Testament was written in the Hebrew language originally. What most of us have in our hands is a translation. Sometimes when a word seems confusing, going back to the original Hebrew word to determine the original meaning and exploring other ways it has been translated can help clarify what the Bible is trying to say. You don't have to be a Hebrew scholar to do this. Several fairly user-friendly tools are available to help, such as a Hebrew/English or Greek/English Bible and Bible dictionaries or lexicons. Using one or two of these, here is what we can learn:

First, the word "wonderfully" is the Hebrew word *palah*,[1] which means to

- Show marvelous.
- Set apart.
- Distinguish.
- Make wonderful.

God made you to be wonderful, marvelous, set apart and distinguished. You are not an accident, a mess or a mistake. Instead, you were created in a wonderful way by a loving Creator. Feels pretty good, right? But what about that "fearfully" word? This Hebrew word (*yare*²) is used hundreds of times in the Old Testament. Most of the time it is translated into some form of the word "fearful," as it was here in Psalms. However, more light shines on the word as we look at other ways it has been translated. How do you feel about the words "awesome" and "reverence"? All three words come together to provide a better understanding of the whole idea.

Think About It

Briefly describe something or somewhere in nature that is both awesome and fearful.

Got something in mind? A couple of my examples would be Niagara Falls and cougars. Both Niagara Falls and cougars are absolutely awesome, lovely creations.

People flock to the falls by droves daily just to stand on the platform and gaze down at the incredible view. How awesome is the power and beauty of this natural wonder! Likewise, cougars are incredibly beautiful animals – sleek, graceful, powerful and gorgeous.

But with both the falls and cougars, an element of fear is very present. No one in his or her right mind would just go running up to the slick edge of this steep waterfall; nor would we go be-bopping up to a sleeping cougar out in the wild and pet him on the head. I hope we would have better sense.

Instead, we would approach the waterfall's edge with caution, respecting the danger near the beauty's edge. And the cougar? Perhaps we view him from the safety of a zoo or from inside a vehicle or on a TV documentary. We are attracted to the beauty and amazed by the awesomeness of the creation, but we always maintain a respectful fear of what can happen with a careless approach.

In this way, we are fearfully made. God created us in an absolutely amazing, awesome way, but an attitude of reverent fearfulness is appropriate in choosing how we approach or use these amazing creations God has given us.

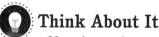 **Think About It**

- Now that we have explored the word "fearfully" (*yare*), how do you think this combination of awesome fearfulness applies to how God created us?

- Have you seen women who present their bodies with carelessness instead of carefulness? What are the consequences?

Recap

The Creator, who is love, has created us in a wonderful way that is absolutely awesome. But with this awesomeness, we recognize that the way we care for our bodies carries an element of cautiousness or fear. If we care for the awesome, wonderful creation (our bodies) in the way the Creator intended, we enjoy an absolutely amazing gift. However, choosing thoughtlessly and carelessly to ignore or abuse this creation of our Lord carries serious and often painful consequences.

Insights From Bethany

I love Psalm 139:1-4: "You know me." I grew up learning the "fearfully and wonderfully made" part in verse 4, but only recently did I truly read verse 1 and let it sink in that God *knows* me in a way that no one else has or ever will. It is immensely comforting and reassuring to me that God intimately *knows* my inner and outer beauty, my good and bad habits, the things that make me smile, the things that make me cry … my happy days, PMS days. He knows me, made me and loves me perfectly and completely.

Now for the next truth.

 Read About It

Jeremiah 29:11

Truth #3: God has a plan for us to give us a hope and a future.

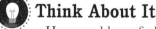 **Think About It**

How would you feel if God were to speak to you directly and say, "I have a plan for *you*"? Would He get your attention? How would you respond?

This has been one of my favorite passages since someone pointed it out to me several years ago. If you are like most folks, you may not have spent much time reading or studying the book of Jeremiah. And certainly, we don't have time to go there in depth now either. But there are some things you've got to know about this passage to really get what God was saying.

Here is the context: God was talking to the Israelites, a people with whom He had a special relationship throughout the Old Testament. These were the folks God delivered out of Egypt and the ones to whom He gave the Promised Land of Canaan. And most important, it was through these people that Jesus came. The Israelites were God's chosen people, descendants of Abraham, and the ancestors of Christ Himself! They had it made! Of course, He had a plan for them.

Ah, but now for the rest of the story. These folks – bathed in the love of God and rescued from slavery under cruel Egyptian taskmasters – responded to their gracious God by completely, totally rejecting Him. And it gets worse. They not only neglected worshiping and honoring Him – that would have been bad enough – but they actually went so far as to start worshiping man-made wood and stone images *instead* of God!

Picture this: God rescued these poor tortured people, who had been beaten down by Egyptian whips and tasks. And He didn't just sneak them out – no! He marched them out after a blaze of power and might. (If you are not familiar with this story, go read about the plagues in Exodus 7:8–12:50.) Unmistakably, this was the mighty hand of God! The Israelites stood on the far banks of the Red Sea rejoicing. God had clearly delivered them with an all-powerful hand!

"Thank You, God! You are wonderful! We love You! You are awesome!" they cried.

Then, "Ooh! Look at the pretty rock! Let's worship it!"

Okay, so it wasn't quite that abrupt, but still, this provides a fairly accurate picture of the end of it all. The Israelites turned their backs on their Deliverer to bow down to images made by human hands and crafted out of rock and wood.

Think About It

• Describe a time when you did something really special for someone else only to have him (or her) turn his back on you. How did you feel? How did you respond?

- How do you think God felt at this point?

How did God respond to all of this? First, He sent prophet after prophet to redirect, teach and warn the Israelites that they were headed in the wrong direction. Repeatedly, He beckoned them back to Him as a mother calls her children back to the safety of her embrace.

Yet Israel ignored Him. So as a good parent disciplines a wayward child, God disciplined Israel. As a result, the Israelites found themselves back in slavery in a strange land under the thumb of a hostile enemy.

Serves them right! It's a wonder God didn't just zap them on the spot, right? Plenty of other people are around; forget Israel! They don't deserve Your love, God! (We humans think like that, don't we?)

But God – our "God is love" God – had a much different approach. God spoke these words recorded in Jeremiah 29:11 to these captured, guilty, undeserving, misdirected, sinful people: "For I know the plans I have for you … plans for welfare and not for evil, to give you a future and a hope" (ESV). This, sisters, is our "God is love" Creator.

Think About It

Put yourself in Israel's shoes for a minute. Imagine yourself in chains – hungry and tired, dirty and depressed – all because you ignored God's love and turned away – and you knew it! Now, picture Him standing in front of you, arms open in love, saying these words from Jeremiah 29. How do you feel? How do you respond?

I can only guess what that would feel like. I can imagine hanging my head in shame as He appeared in the doorway. Maybe I would even pull back into the shadows as He approached, knowing what I deserved. But then as He began talking, offering His words of love and hope, I can imagine my surprise and downright shock. "Are you serious? Are you talking to *me*? You mean You still love me? Still open Your arms to welcome me?" As I reach for Him, the shackles release, and I bury my head in His embrace, crying through tears for His forgiveness. "I am so sorry, Lord! How could I ever have forgotten You? Please, please forgive me! I love You, Lord! I will never turn away again. I will seek You with my *whole* heart!"

Been there? Maybe not in a literal prison, but you have probably been in a prison of your own making, crafted from your own sin. We've all been there and maybe still are there. Sometimes we feel so hopeless.

Read About It
- Psalm 102:27
- James 1:17

Think About It
- What do these verses have to say about the nature of God?

- Given His unchanging nature, what can we learn about Him in how He treated Israel?

- Because He is unchanging, how do you think He will treat us?

Read About It
Jeremiah 29:12-13

Think About It
- In these verses, God describes a response of His people that He will honor. What is it?

- How would that look in your daily life?

Somebody out there is thinking: "Yes, but that promise of a plan, hope and future wasn't made to me. It was made to the Israelites." So let's explore.

You are right. This passage in Jeremiah 29 was written specifically to the Israelites about a specific situation they were facing. So what about us today? Does God have a plan for us today, or was that just a back-then promise?

Read About It
- John 10:10
- John 20:31
- 1 Timothy 4:8

Think About It

- What do you see in these verses that mirrors what God said to the Israelites?

- Are these promises just about heaven, or do they say something about this life too? (Take another look at 1 Timothy 4:8 if you aren't sure.) Why does that matter?

- What words or phrases in these verses talk about a plan? a hope? a future?

- How do these promises make you feel?

This same God who reached down into the slavery pit that engulfed the Israelites and offered them a hope and a future has plans for us today to give us an abundant life both on earth and in heaven. What a glorious promise! And because He is unchanging, we can be assured that He will keep His promises to us just as He has throughout the ages with all of His children.

Summing It Up

We are made in the image of our love-light-spirit God who always seeks our best. Always. And being made in His image, we carry the beauty of our Creator (**Truth #1**). We were fearfully and wonderfully made by Him and, therefore, must treat our bodies with great care as our Maker intended (**Truth #2**). This same God has known you personally from before you even knew yourself, and He loves you dearly. And just as He assured the Israelites, God has a plan to give *you* a hope and a future (**Truth #3**). We can always thank God in advance for what He is going to do in our lives because we know that it is going to be good.

Think About It

Who better than the One who loves you to guide you? Who better than the One who designed and created you to write the owner's manual for your care? Who better than a loving Creator to lay before you a path of hope and a path to a positive future? Given all of this, will you trust God's guidance?

Talk About It

1. In general, what makes trusting someone easy or hard?

2. How is trusting God similar to and different from trusting a person in our lives?

3. Who is the best person to write an owner's manual for a creation? How do you feel about the idea of God writing your owner's manual? Why is your Creator the best One to write your owner's manual?

4. The Israelites were drawn away by what was popular in their culture: idolatry. What things in your culture today try to distract you or draw you away from God's plan? What are steps you can take to help keep your focus on God?

Pray About It

Loving Creator, help me trust You more. You alone know how I was crafted in my mother's womb. You alone know who I am in my deepest parts. You alone know the plan that is best for me. Help me cling to You and seek You with my whole heart. I long to find You.

Recommended Reading

Redeeming Love by Francine Rivers (Colorado Springs: Multonomah, 2005). This novel retells the story of the prophet Hosea in the context of the California Gold Rush. The prophet Hosea (Michael Hosea in the novel) follows God's instruction to take a hardened prostitute (Gomer in the Bible, Angel in the novel) as his wife. In the Bible, God used this real-life example of unconditional, redeeming love as a picture of His love for idolatrous Israel. Francine Rivers artfully tells this story from Angel's point of view. Although this is fiction, the perspective brings light to what it means to be beautiful and loved by the Creator.

Chapter 3

I Love ...

Starting Point

*T*his is a timed exercise. Give yourself 30 seconds to complete this sentence in at least 20 different ways: I love _____. (You may want to do this on a separate sheet of paper.) Ready? Go!

Did you get 20 answers? more than 20? If you got at least 20, you probably have a pretty wide assortment of things on your list. My entries spanned from special people to spiritual realms to favorite foods, places and activities. I love lots of people, places and things! Isn't God great for designing our bodies to enjoy the wonderful world He created? What a great package with lots to love!

Opening Reflections

Let's go down a little side trail for a minute that will lead back into this journey on love. God, in His incredible wisdom, selected a unique language for the writing of the New Testament books. This language, Koine Greek, is a specific dialect within the Greek language that is no longer spoken. It is a dead language, meaning that no countries use it for day-to-day communication anymore.

God's selection of this language is relevant to this study for at least two reasons. (1) Koine Greek is a very specific language, meaning that words don't tend to have a bazillion unrelated meanings for the same word. Instead, the language has many words to express different ideas or concepts. (2) The fact that it is a dead language means that it is a settled language. To understand the significance of this, let's think about the English language for a minute.

English is a living language because living people are actively using it every day for communication. Because it is still in use, it is constantly changing. Just ask anyone over the age of 40 what these words or phrases meant when she was a kid, and compare her answers to what they commonly mean today:

- Copy and paste
- Disk
- Print
- Crib
- Port
- Spam
- Web

Do you know all of the then and now definitions? That is the nature of a living language – it changes. However, because Koine Greek is not a living language but a dead one, it does *not* continue to change. That means what words meant at the time in which they were written is what they mean now. That will be very important as we study further.

Think About It

Can you think of other words that have changed meaning in the past few years?

Now, let's go back to the word "love" armed with these important perspectives. Think about the first concept about Koine Greek: It is a very specific language. In our language, we might say we love our parents, love our best friend, love our pet dog Rover, love pizza, and love watching sunsets. The Greeks, however, would never have used the same word to describe each of these relationships.

Instead, they would have drawn from their very specific language to use a very specific word for each of those relationships. In fact, just to describe human relations alone required four very different words. That doesn't even include pets, pizza, sunsets or whatever other things we might list. Understanding these differences is vital to this study of what God says about love because examining which word God used in different places will clarify His messages to us.

As noted above, the Greeks used four different words to talk about love in human relationships. Three appear in the New Testament, and the one that does not directly appear is referenced using other related words. Here are the four words:

(1) Eros [1] – This is the one word for human love that is not actually used in the New Testament. However, the thought is there in some different ways. Recognizing, though, that the Greeks had this separate word is important because we don't often make this distinction in our language today. The word *eros* means sexual affection, such as between husband and wife. It is not limited to just sexual intercourse, but instead describes the physical, sexual affection within a mutual relationship.

In other words, *eros* specifically is talking about sexual love. The Bible does not use this word, but it does refer to the husband-wife sexual relationship (*eros*) indirectly in several places, like we do in English. For instance, we might say two people are "sleeping together" to talk about this relationship while the New Testament talks about "the marriage bed" (Hebrews 13:4) or a husband and wife "com[ing] together" (1 Corinthians 7:5). God created and condones this expression of sexual love within a marriage relationship.

(2) Phileo [2] – This is the word the Greeks would have used to talk about friendships. Had you lived back then, you would have said you *phileo* your best friend. That means you have a fondness for or like being with that person. You both like each other and feel emotionally close, meaning the relationship is mutually shared. You would have used this word to talk about people to whom you feel emotionally attached – your friends.

(3) Storge [3] – Greeks would have used this word when talking about the relationship they had with their families. This word described the bond with brothers, sisters, mothers, fathers, aunts, uncles and such. The emotional bond exists because you are family. You share a home, a heritage and a history that helps you feel close to one another. Like *eros* and *phileo*, *storge* carries with it the idea of a mutually shared closeness.

(4) *Agape* [4] – This kind of love is different from the other three. First, it is unconditional. You know that people's feelings about friends, family and even sexual relations change with time. You see it every day. "Jane isn't my friend anymore." "I can't stand my brother." Marriages break up, and people walk away from the most intimate physical relationships they will ever experience.

One of the reasons this happens is because the first three kinds of love (*phileo*, *storge* and *eros*) are based in part on emotions, and emotions change depending on how you treat one another, moods at the moment, other stresses in one another's lives, and a zillion other influences. Also, these three kinds of love, by design, involve a mutual relationship. For example, being best friends with someone who doesn't like you or want to be around you is hard at best and unlikely because being best friends implies a shared relationship. Likewise, you can't very easily be family with a brother or sister who moves away and refuses to have contact with you again.

But *agape* is different. It remains constant regardless of what is happening around you or the other person. The key difference is that *agape* is not based on emotion but, instead, is based on a decision – a choice. *Agape* says, "I will love you no matter what."

Agape is a decision to do what is best for another person over time regardless of feelings or emotions (yours or theirs). This means, then, that *agape* does not have to be mutual to exist. For instance, if I decide to do what is best for you over time regardless of how I feel about it (*agape*), I can keep my decision firm even if you don't like me or even if you choose to be unkind to me. My decision to *agape* you is not dependent on a mutual relationship. You can hate my guts, and I can still *agape* you. That doesn't always mean I have to feel great toward you or you toward me. It just means my decision to treat you with love is firmly established, no matter what.

This, of course, is the kind of love God has for us.

 **Read About It**
Romans 5:9-10

Think About It

What kind of love is this passage describing? How do you know?

We did not know God when He chose to send His Son. Nor did we know His Son when He chose to die. In fact, we weren't even born yet. However, God and His Son chose to love (*agape*) us before we even existed!

So how does *agape* look in our lives today? Remember, *agape* means choosing what is best for the other person over time regardless of feelings. *Agape* in action …

• Gets a mom to take her newborn baby for an immunization shot although they both will cry.

• Helps a mom say no to little girls who want ice cream instead of supper.

• Gives a girl courage to stand up to the bully at school who is picking on a smaller child, even though she is afraid the bully will turn on her.

• Says, "I love you enough to wait for you."

• Nurses a sick child or spouse through a long terminal illness.

Think About It

What are some other examples where you have seen *agape* demonstrated?

Let's take a few minutes to explore another powerful example of the importance of distinction among the various Greek words we might call "love."

Read About It

John 21:15-17

Do these verses puzzle you? Do you wonder why Jesus kept asking Peter the same question after he answered Him? I puzzled over this for years before looking at what they both *really* said. Let's read it again with the Greek words inserted.

> So when they had finished breakfast, Jesus said to Simon Peter, "Simon, son of John, do you love [**agape**] Me more than these?" [Peter] said to Him, "Yes, Lord; You know that I love [**phileo**] You." [Jesus] said to him, "Tend My lambs."

> [Jesus] said to him a second time, "Simon, son of John, do you love [**agape**] Me?" [Peter] said to Him, "Yes, Lord;

You know that I love [*phileo*] you." [Jesus] said to him, "Shepherd My sheep."

[Jesus] said to him the third time, "Simon son of John, do you love [*phileo*] Me?" Peter was grieved because He said to him the third time, "Do you love [*phileo*] Me?" And he said to Him, "Lord, You know all things; You know that I love [*phileo*] You." Jesus said to him, "Tend My sheep."

You see, on the surface of the English translation, which uses the overarching word "love" all the way through, we miss a very deep meaningful exchange between Peter and our Lord.

Think About It

- What is the difference between what Jesus asked and what Peter answered? Why does that matter?

- What was different about what Jesus asked Peter the third time? Why do you think Peter was hurt by that altered question?

- Why does thinking through the kinds of love we have toward others and the kinds others have toward us matter?

Although we have drawn lines distinguishing these four different kinds of love that people can have for one another, it is also important to know that you can have more than one of them overlapping at a time. For instance, I may have a best friend (*phileo*) whom I choose to treat with *agape* love. That means, for now at least, we have a mutual friendship and enjoy each other. In addition to that, I have made a decision to continue to do what is best for that person even if the situation changes and this person no longer wants to be my friend.

Think About It

Think about these combinations. What would these relationships look like?

- *Phileo* + *Storge* = _____.
- *Storge* + *Agape* = _____.
- *Eros* + *Agape* = _____.

What is the only relationship in which all four kinds of love can exist at the same time? Why?

Summing It Up

As we continue walking down our paths as women of God, these definitions of love will play an important role. By thinking through all of the stuff that our culture calls love, we will be able to recognize what is really going on in our hearts and minds and in the relationships around us. This will help us make choices that not only lead us to loving others better but also help us to recognize when someone is truly loving us.

Talk About It

1. Give some examples from TV shows or movies you have seen where you could clearly see one or more of these four kinds of love demonstrated. How did you know which kind of love it was?

2. *Phileo, storge, eros* and *agape* together are God's ultimate package deal for marriage. Why do you think God designed all four to be in marriage? What would happen if one of them was missing?

3. Can a relationship survive long-term without *agape*? Why, or why not?

Pray About It

Thank You, our loving God, for Your generous *agape* love. Without it, we would have no hope. Help us to open our eyes to true love and to understand Your *agape* heart so that we can become more like You.

Recommended Reading

Love Life for Every Married Couple: How to Fall in Love, Stay in Love, Rekindle Your Love by Ed Wheat and Gloria Okes Perkins (Grand Rapids: Zondervan, 1997). As the title indicates, this book was written for married couples. This book was one of the first that my husband and I read after getting married. It was a huge aha moment for me in really grasping the difference in having *agape* love in a relationship versus the other three types of love.

Chapter 4

Woman

Recap

So far, we've explored some foundational truths that provide a context for God's guidance. Let's review. Because God is our love-light-spirit Father, He will always choose what is best for us and right for us with an eye to what will matter most over time. It is this same God who created us fearfully and wonderfully in His image and with a plan to give us an abundant life, a hope, and a future. This *agape*-loving Father always knows and always chooses what is best for us. So when He does give us direction and guidance, we can set our feet securely on that path, knowing that it is the right path and that it will lead us to His plan for our lives. What a marvelous gift!

With all of this in mind, we will begin exploring some of what this amazing God has set before us. As we progress into the next few lessons, we will begin to see how His wisdom and love play out in the guidance He has offered. We will begin by exploring God's plan in designing us as women.

Opening Reflections

The ways in which the world views a woman's worth have changed significantly just in my lifetime. Beginning with the women's liberation movement in the '70s, women have been encouraged (sometimes even pressured) to compete with men in every sense of the word. The Bible, at times, is viewed as outdated or behind the times in the way it portrays women and their roles. However, our masterful Creator would, of course, disagree. Let's take a deep look at what He says about women, the crowning object of His created world.

Starting Point

What do you like about being a woman?

Woman was the last created being as described in the first two chapters of Genesis. The sequence of events leading up to her creation gives us a picture of the value God placed on her role in His world. Let's start by exploring how God framed women from the beginning. Let's begin our exploration with a math lesson.

Read About It
Genesis 1

Think About It
Record the number of times God saw that something was good in this first chapter of His message.

Read About It
Genesis 2:18

Think About It
• In this verse, God said something was not good. What was it?

• What did God say He was planning to do about it?

Right after God stated that something was not good and even stated what He planned to do about it, He did something that seems a bit odd on the surface. Notice that instead of getting right to the task of making Adam's companion, God gave Adam a job to do. He brought every animal to Adam for him to name.

Read About It
Genesis 2:19-20

Notice that after the animal-naming parade, verse 20 restates what God had already said in verse 18: "But for Adam there was not found a helper suitable for him."

Think About It

Why do you think God chose this timing to march all of these animals past Adam?

We know that God wasn't hoping Adam would find a helper among the beasts because He had already said in verse 18 that He was going to make a helper suitable for Adam. The Bible doesn't tell us for sure why God chose this time for Adam to name the animals, but we do know that God created Adam and knew exactly what He needed (as He does for us today). So perhaps this was an exercise for Adam's benefit to prepare him for the incredible gift he was about to receive.

Imagine for a moment that you are Adam. God sets you down in a comfortable spot and starts moving every creature He created past you, one at a time. "Okay, Adam, take a good look at this one, and give it a name." (How would you have liked that job?) And this was not a rushed process, because Adam had to take time to name each one as it went by. See him sitting there? "Elephant, aardvark, giraffe ..." He did this for every single one. I imagine that took a while. And at the end (v. 20), we see the echoed statement of God from verse 18. Adam needs a helpmeet.

Now, God already knew that He was going to make Adam a helpmeet. So maybe, just maybe, God set aside this time for Adam to realize the hole in his life without the special creation that God was about to fashion. Imagine Adam at the end of this process. Perhaps he sat back, a little weary, sure, but in absolute awe over the many creatures God had shown him. They were all sizes, all shapes – smooth ones, furry ones. He had seen them all. Yet as amazing as that all was, none of them was fashioned to fit with Adam – not physically, not emotionally, not intellectually. Now he was ready for God's gift.

So God put Adam to sleep – probably a much needed rest at this point, don't you think? And when God awakened His sleeping creation, here was this amazing form before Adam's eyes. Like him, but different – very different! Some differences were obvious at first sight, but other differences were deeply embedded into her very nature and design. She, like Adam, was created for a specific purpose. And while she complemented Adam in design, she was not identical to him. She was unique – on purpose. Of all of God's amazing handiwork, this crowning creation of the unique, carefully crafted man and woman pair was the climax.

 Think About It

• How are you feeling about yourself as a woman right now?

• In what ways are women specifically unique and different from anything else in God's creation?

• Whom do you think of as the ideal woman – someone you look up to and admire? What are her characteristics? What does she have to offer others?

Look a little further into what God said here in these few short verses. What does it mean to be a helpmeet or a suitable helper? To understand this better, let's take another quick side lesson. You may remember from our discussion of love that the New Testament was written in Koine Greek. The Old Testament, though, was written in the Hebrew language. So to dig a little deeper into the Old Testament, we will explore the original meanings of words in Hebrew.

Depending on the Bible version you are using, you may see Genesis 2:18 translated in different ways. The King James Version, for example, says that God planned to create a "help meet." The word translated "help" here is a simple little Hebrew word: *ezer*. [1] The English translation of "help" is pretty good as a single-word translation. To take it a little deeper, we would add "to surround, to protect or aid."

Another way to learn about what words mean is by looking at other ways a word was used in the Bible. The Hebrew word *ezer* was used only 21 times in the entire Old Testament. Two of those times are in these verses we've been exploring. Three times, the word was used to talk about someone who either wasn't helping when he should have been or about someone who was helping on the wrong side – helping evil. For the remaining 16 times, the word was used to describe how God Himself cares for us. This is a very powerful kind of help.

Read About It

- Psalm 33:20
- Psalm 121:1-2
- Psalm 146:5-6

Think About It

- What do you think the word "help" (*ezer*) means in these verses?

- Describe how that help looks.

- How is God our *ezer*?

This word carries with it a lot of protection, gentleness and support. It is *not* a word indicating that females are lesser people; women are not just the man's "help staff" around the house. Instead, this is an active, supportive and protective role.

To illustrate, have you ever tried to pick up or pet a tiny baby animal such as a tiny bird in a nest or a newborn kitten? You can lose a hand! The animal's mother is being an *ezer*. You had better leave her babies alone!

Yet that same mama cat, for instance, will ever so gently pick up that baby kitten and snuggle it, nurse it and groom it. That, too, is what an *ezer* does. That unique blend of gentleness and fierceness that a woman feels when protecting someone she loves is a pretty clear picture of the role God formed her to fill.

The other word here, "meet" (*neged* [2] in the Hebrew), is much more common. Used 114 times in the Old Testament, it means "mate, opposite, counterpart, in front of, to stand out boldly opposite." The idea here is something being connected to something else, yet being uniquely different from it – not alike, but a completer or complement.

Man and woman are not alike. Yet within the human race, each is important. Men bring certain traits into our home, family, community and world that women do not have. Likewise, women bring qualities into the home, family, community and world that do not come from men. We are completers of one another.

To illustrate this concept of complements or completers, suppose you have a brand new nut and bolt, perfectly formed in every way. No nicks, stains or damage. They are both designed and created to fill a specific purpose together. Yet they do not look alike. It is easy to see which is which. They are each fashioned to fill different roles, so when the strengths of one are combined correctly with the strengths of the other, they form a new unique role that neither of them could accomplish alone.

Think About It

Think of an example of two things that are different, yet they cannot work without each other. What would one do without the other?

Now, please understand this point. We are exploring God's wisdom in fashioning men and women differently for their different roles. Although part of His design relates to the roles He plans for a man and woman to take in marriage, this concept does not mean that a man has to get married to be complete. Nor does it mean that a woman has to find a man to be complete. It does mean, however, that God knew what He was doing in creating men and women as uniquely different beings.

We all have different roles to play in life and different responsibilities to carry, regardless of whether we are married. God fashioned both men and women in such a way as to best be able to carry the responsibilities He would lay on each one's shoulders, whether they choose to be single or married. As we continue our study of God's plan, we will explore this concept further. But for now, simply recognize that you – a woman of God – were created by a loving Father for a unique and powerful purpose. You hold unique qualities that no man possesses. You are woman.

Summing It Up

To say that God knew what He was doing in creating males and females as He did would be a vast understatement. As we move forward to dig deeper into His unique designs and our unique roles, we will again be amazed by God's infinite wisdom in creating us to be exactly what we need to be for the life He envisions for us. What an incredible journey!

Talk About It

1. How does this biblical view of a woman as a helpmeet (*ezer, neged*) differ from the world's view of a woman's role?

2. Do the different roles God designed for men and women mean they are not equal?

3. What are some of the lies that the world would have us believe about the idea of being a helpmeet?

4. What can we learn from God's role as an *ezer* that can help us fulfill our roles as an *ezer* in the lives of those around us?

Pray About It

Lord, thank You for fashioning us as women into our unique designs. Help us, Lord, to truly be an *ezer* – a helper, comforter, supporter – to those around us each day. We thank You, Lord, that You are our *ezer*. Without You, we would be forever hopeless and lost. You give us meaning and purpose. We praise You and thank You.

Chapter 5

The Gift

Opening Reflections

Several years ago, I was attending a home demonstration party. (You know the kind, where you go to a friend's house and watch a distributor demonstrate products that you can then purchase.) At this particular party, the distributor was allowing all of the guests to pick a door prize from a large bowl of kitchen gadgets. The few recognizable items with a clear purpose were rapidly snatched up. Most of the items, though, had us all puzzled. Clearly, they were all intended to be good things because they were offered as door prizes.

Finally, after a few minutes of shuffling through the remaining contents looking for something with a familiar purpose, we began holding up the strange items and asking how they could be used. Now, our eyes were opened! We began selecting these wonderful answers to modern kitchen problems, which only moments earlier were useless, unwanted items. Understanding purpose is one important element in recognizing value.

Starting Point

Suppose you were given an object that you had never seen before. How would you determine whether it was valuable?

There are probably a lot of ways you might determine an object's value. Here are some of the ideas I had. First, how I got the object would be a clue to me. Did I get it as a special gift from someone who loves me? Was it presented in a special package? gift-wrapped? If so, I'd probably guess right up front that this was at least intended to be a special gift of value.

Second, I'd probably determine its value by its purpose. Now, at this point, I may have to ask: "Wow! Thanks! Um … what is it? How do I use it?" Maybe, too, I would take a cue from any similarities it shared with other objects that were familiar to me. "It kind of looks like a … ."

Then, the object's value to me would partly depend on whether I was able to (or wanted to) use it in my life. For instance, suppose someone gave me a gun. I personally have no interest in shooting anything in my current circumstances. However, if I were lost out in the woods and had to survive on my own for a period of time, a gun would be of great value to me, assuming I knew something about how to use it correctly so I didn't end up shooting off my big toe or something worse.

So the value of a gift comes from the giver, its purpose and its usefulness in my life, among other things that you might have named.

Now to our study of God's Word. At the end of the previous lesson, Adam had just named all the animals in God's creation and discovered a void in his life that God had filled with a helpmeet. As we move forward in this lesson, we will unfold some of the details of this gift.

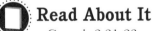 **Read About It**
Genesis 2:21-23

 **Think About It**
God formed Adam out of the dust of the earth (Genesis 2:7) as He had all of the animals and birds (v. 19). But Eve was formed from part of man. Why do you think that is important?

The Bible doesn't tell us exactly why God chose this method to create Eve, but what we do learn is that Adam recognized her as a part of him, taken from him. So as he awakened from the sleep God provided him during this process, Adam was given a gift. He knew the source of the gift and recognized the connection to himself (Genesis 2:23). The question to ask, then, was "What am I supposed to do with this gift?"

One thing that is striking here is that God immediately provided Adam with some guidelines on how to use the gift he had just received. This, again, is evidence of God's completeness in providing what we need. God didn't wait days, months or years to give Adam what he needed. Instead, God immediately provided for his need and gave Adam the instructions on how to use the gift wisely.

 ## Read About It
Genesis 2:24

 ## Think About It

- Have you ever gotten a complex gift and jumped into using it before reading the instruction manual? What were the results?

- Why do we need instruction manuals?

- Did God provide us with an instruction manual for life? Explain.

I have had several times in my life when I've gotten a complicated tool or piece of equipment and just turned it on and tried to figure it out as I went. Right now, I have a cellphone with all kinds of buttons and features I don't have a clue how to operate. Sometimes my lack of patience in reading the instructions that the tool's creator prepared for me has resulted in accidentally breaking something or at least not using the object to its full potential. Many times I have found myself saying "Oh! I didn't know it would do that" months after receiving a gift. We end up making work harder, blundering through mistakes, and missing important benefits when we get in too big of a hurry to check out and follow instructions provided by the designer.

So exploring God's instruction manual on the family is vital to experiencing the many blessings God designed. All of us are in families of some sort. As we continue through these chapters together, some may find places where their families match the plan and some may find places where things don't match. Keep in mind that God is describing what He *intended* for the family to be. This is our love-light-spirit God. What He says to us is always in our best interest, out of love, and with an eye on the future.

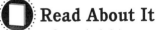 Read About It

Genesis 2:24

Think About It

In this verse, God laid the foundation for what He intended marriage to be. What did He say?

Three important concepts are presented here. (1) God said that a man should leave his father and his mother. One reason this is important is because it tells us that God is setting a principle for all time, not just talking to Adam and Eve. How do we know? Well, neither Adam nor Eve had a mother or father. Adam and Eve didn't really even know what it was to be a mom or dad yet. So God had to be setting a permanent standard for establishing the human home. (We'll see more proof of that in a few minutes.)

(2) God understood that a man and woman would, under normal circumstances, have a strong tie to their own parents. So here, in this short phrase, God established that a husband and wife will need to move from having their parents as their strongest family ties to having each other as their new family unit. This doesn't mean that the couple can never speak to their parents again, but it does showcase the new bond created in marriage – a bond intended to surpass that in all other human relationships.

(3) Man is to "cleave unto his wife: and they shall be one flesh" (KJV). This concept is closely related to the second. The word "cleave" carries the idea of bonding together. This is not merely being next to each other; instead, it is becoming one. It is a joining together to the point that you cannot separate the two without damaging both. The closeness expressed here is intended to bring two individuals together as one newly formed being. This bond, then, becomes the strongest human bond in both the husband's and wife's lives. No other human relationship is to be stronger.

Think About It

- Why do you think God specifically noted that the husband is to leave his mother and father before cleaving to his wife?

- Do you know couples who seem to have followed these guidelines well? What does that look like?

• Do you know couples who seem to struggle with these principles? How do you see that demonstrated?

Let's examine even more evidence that the principles in this short, little verse are God's instructions for all families for all time.

Read About It
Matthew 19:3-6

Think About It

• Why do you think it is significant that Jesus quoted Genesis 2:24?

• What other important note did He add in the last half of Matthew 19:6? Why is this important?

In Matthew 19:3-6, Jesus was responding to a question that the Pharisees asked. In His response, He quoted Genesis 2:24, which we have been studying. Notice the context of these few verses. In Matthew 19:3, we see that the purpose of the Pharisees' question was to tempt Jesus. They were trying to set a trap for Him by what they asked. Jesus, in response, returned to the original family "owner's manual" to restate the truth God provided to Adam and Eve from the beginning.

Just a quick historical and cultural side note: The Pharisees were asking if it was okay for a husband to divorce (or put away) his wife for any reason. At this time in history, women, by law (human government law), were not allowed to seek a divorce. Only men could seek a divorce. That is why this question was asked from the husband's point of view. However, the principle God established and Jesus restated stands for both husband and wife.

Jesus' answer came straight from the "owner's manual." That should not surprise us because God and His Son are on the same page (John 14:8-11). Jesus reminded the Pharisees of what was written already regarding this question, quoting from Genesis 1:27 and Genesis 2:24.

Think About It

What can we learn from the way Jesus answered this question, which was intended to trap or tempt Him?

In Matthew 19:6, Jesus added an important insight: "What therefore God has joined together, let no man separate." Notice who does the joining according to this verse. God Himself takes on the role of the One joining a husband and wife in marriage. It is His hand that connects the two, creating a new "one flesh" union. We will explore some of the ways He does this later.

Jesus included a warning here too: "let no man separate." So God intended a husband and wife to set their relationship above all other human relationships (leave) and join together with each other (cleave). As God sets His seal on the couple so as to make them one, Jesus warned that humans are not to separate what God has joined. This is intended to be a "till death do us part" relationship. Not satisfied with Jesus' answer, the Pharisees countered with another question.

 Read About It
Matthew 19:7

 Think About It
Are there times when God lays out a truth in our lives and we are tempted to say, "Yes, but what about _____?" Why is that the case?

The Pharisees noted something that was true for their culture. There was a time period in the Israelite's history when divorce was a more common practice than the original "owner's manual" instructed. Jesus acknowledged that fact, but then sets the record straight on God's original expectation.

 Read About It
Matthew 19:8

 Think About It
• Why did Jesus say Moses permitted divorce?

• What does it mean to have a "hard heart"?

• What attitudes do you see in our culture today toward marriage? How do you think that may compare to what was said about divorce during Moses' day?

• What do you think Jesus meant by "from the beginning it has not been this way" (v. 8)?

So we can see that Moses, who was the human leader of the Israelites as they moved from Egyptian slavery to the land of Canaan, allowed divorce. I like the word that the King James Version uses here: "Moses … *suffered* you to put away your wives" (emphasis added). Moses was a godly man. I would imagine that it grieved him to see the Israelites go against what was intended from the beginning. To an even greater extent, it grieves God when we choose to follow our own paths instead of His. Jesus took this concept one step further.

Read About It
Matthew 19:9

Think About It
What does "except" mean? What is the exception in this verse?

Let's start by defining a couple of words because they, like the word "love" in the Greek, have very specific meanings. First, consider the word Jesus used in His exception for divorce: "immorality." (Your translation may use "marital unfaithfulness" or "fornication.") This word is translated from the Greek word *porneia*. [1] A hint to its meaning is in our related English word "pornography." It involves sexual behavior with someone other than your spouse (husband or wife). It is specifically talking about having sexual activity outside of a marriage bond. The second word, "adultery" (*moichao* [2]), is also important to understand. Adultery means a married person is having sexual relations with someone besides her spouse.

Now, let's start putting this together. First – just for a moment – let's take the exception out and consider the guideline Jesus is presenting: "Whoever divorces his wife … and marries another woman commits adultery."

Now, remember that "adultery" means someone who is having inappropriate sex while married. So why is divorcing and remarrying a problem? Because God joined the husband and wife, and neither of them has God's permission to separate this union. So the husband is still married in God's eyes even if he divorces his wife. And the wife is not off the hook either. In the New King James Version, Jesus explained: "And whoever marries her who is divorced commits adultery." You see, when God joins a couple as one flesh, He intends them to stay that way. He made that very clear.

Read About It
Malachi 2:14-16

Some of this passage is a little hard to understand, but some of it is not. God is talking about the husband and wife relationship (v. 14). Verse 15 is kind of hard to grasp, but the beginning of verse 16 lays out the bottom line: God hates divorce.

Insights From Bethany

Divorce is not only hated by God, but it also deeply saddens God – even more than it hurts and saddens me. When Scripture says that He hates divorce, He's not coldly turning away in disgust and dismissal. Rather, He is turning His tear-filled eyes toward our hearts and is forced to see them – the beautiful hearts He has created to fit into each other – brutally and messily ripped apart. How could He not hate that? It is barely akin to our witnessing of a newly bloomed flower being crushed, a painted masterpiece of a sweeping landscape going up in flames, or a creation of priceless value being irrevocably destroyed. That is divorce.

Think About It
• Why do you think God hates divorce?

• What is a covenant? What is a covenant based on? Emotion? Decision?

• What do you think is significant about the idea of marriage being a covenant relationship?

Now, let's go back to the exception we set aside a few minutes ago. Jesus established the principle to those asking about divorce that God intends marriage to be a lifelong, one-flesh commitment. He does, however, allow for one single exception to the lifelong covenant: fornication. In other words, if one of the marriage partners should step outside of the marriage relationship and have sexual relations with someone else, God allows an exception of divorce for this tremendous wound to the marriage. This is, though, the only exception that Jesus presented. So other statements made in the Bible regarding marriage must align with what He said here. God's Word does not contain contradictions.

And so human nature sets in. "But what if …" And we can think of a thousand situations. Yet according to Jesus, "from the beginning it has not been this way" (Matthew 19:8). From the very beginning, God set a pattern in place, and it was for this pattern that He designed us. What is important for us to realize is that God designed marriage from the beginning to be one man and one woman that He Himself joined together in one flesh for life. That is the foundational instruction in God's manual for this amazing gift of the family. When we misuse or mishandle the gift, pain and disappointment result. In the following chapters, we will explore how God actually designed us with this pattern in mind – an absolutely amazing study of God's wisdom!

Summing It Up

God has a plan for the family. He had this plan from the beginning when He presented the first husband with the first wife. The plan remains today, as Christ verified during His ministry on this earth. His plan is one man and one woman cleaving and bonding together for life.

Talk About It

1. Whom do you know who seems to have a happy marriage? What evidence do you see? How does that couple speak to each other? How are love and respect demonstrated?

2. What are some of the painful results of divorce? Who suffers?

3. What happens if a husband or wife clings to another relationship (parents, friends, children) more than to his or her spouse?

4. How can a husband and wife protect their marriage bond?

5. What messages are here for single women who may want to marry in the future?

Pray About It

Lord, our world encourages us to throw away our marriages. Please, Lord, give us wisdom and strength to hold to Your will and Your pattern for our families. Please strengthen the covenant relationship of marriage within our homes and hearts and within Your church so that we will not tire of upholding its holiness and beauty to the world around us. We thank You for providing us with guidance in this life.

Supplemental Thoughts

It is beyond the scope of this chapter to answer every nuance of human existence, and it would be a mistake to try to do so without adequate space and time. Yet here are some passages that may help those who are challenged by other questions or situations.

What God says to …

• Single adults: 1 Corinthians 7:8-9 (Paul, the author of this epistle, was not married).

• Widowed adults: 1 Corinthians 7:39.

• Married couples who cannot live together (perhaps there is abuse or some other situation that is threatening): 1 Corinthians 7:10-11.

• Adults whose spouse is not a believer: 1 Corinthians 7:12-14.

• Adults whose spouse abandons the family: 1 Corinthians 7:15. (Note that the idea of "not [being] under bondage" is not the same idea as being divorced. The Greek word translated "bondage" means "slave," indicating that a spouse is not a slave to follow after the one who leaves. Keep in mind, though, that this verse does not contradict what Jesus said in Matthew 19 about marriage and divorce. They have to fit together.)

• Adults who struggle with homosexuality: Romans 1:26-27.

Chapter 6

Guys and Girls Are Different, Part One

Opening Reflections

I have been canoeing three times in my life thus far. The first time, I was a teenager and was paired in a canoe with a new girl who had recently joined our church youth group. We did not know each other well at all. Needless to say, we experienced a lot of bumps, jolts and tumbles as we struggled to work out our game plan. A few feet away from the take-out point, we flipped the canoe and went flying down a 5-foot drop without our canoe. This experience underscored in a very practical sense the importance of sharing a clear purpose, establishing roles, and having clean communication lines.

Starting Point

Have you ever been canoeing down a river or creek? Regardless of whether you have, what do you know about keeping the canoe upright in the water and headed in the direction you want it to go?

Bookmark those thoughts. We'll come back.

Countless books, TV documentaries, movies and magazine articles have been written exploring and explaining how guys and girls are different. None of us doubt that there are differences, but we may not all have a clear understanding of just how very different we are.

We explored in a previous lesson how God intentionally created woman as a counterpart for or completer for man. Women are designed in every way to complement, not duplicate men. Much like jigsaw puzzle pieces, we are formed and designed differently, yet in such a way that we fit together to form God's picture of the family.

From the very creation of woman, it was clear that she was different. God called her a "completer" (Hebrew: *neged*). He formed her from Adam instead of from the dust of the earth. At first glance, Adam could see that she was physically different from him. Yet the wisdom of God's design in creating both male and female goes way beyond the obvious physical differences.

Chapters 6 and 7 will explore some of these differences and how they work within God's plan. As we look at these differences, I want to explore with you the immeasurable wisdom of our Creator by looking at how these differences enhance our ability to fulfill the roles He has assigned to each gender. Let's start by getting a sense of these roles.

 ## Read About It
Ephesians 5:23-33

 ## Think About It
- What role is clearly defined in this passage for the husband?

- What comparison did God provide to help clarify what He meant?

- What characteristics of leadership does that comparison imply?

- How does this model of leadership in the home differ from the world's view?

God clearly placed man in the role of head of the family. This is not a position of dominance or selfishness. Instead, God painted a picture of how Christ is the head of the church and compared the husband and wife roles in the home to this relationship. As we have studied together in previous lessons, accepting the leadership of Christ is easy when we realize that it is motivated by love. That is the spirit from which a husband is to lead his wife within God's design.

So what is a woman's primary role?

Read About It

- Genesis 2:18
- Titus 2:3-5

We have already studied together in detail the role the wife has as a helper/completer of her husband. The passage in Titus provides some clarity into other specific roles and responsibilities the woman shoulders.

Think About It

- List the roles of women recorded in Titus.

- How do these roles help or complete a male's leadership role?

- How do these roles strengthen the family?

Now, let's go back to the canoe. Granted, my three experiences canoeing make me far from an expert. However, there are a few things I've figured out even with just a little bit of experience. For instance, if you have two people paddling in a canoe, they had better be in agreement on where they want to go. Also, the person in the front had better be paying attention to obstacles like rocks and logs and such in the path ahead. Adding to that, aiming the canoe downstream from the beginning is a lot better than getting sideways in the water. Finally, going down rough waters backward is really not much fun at all. Add in a couple of kids, a bunch of gear, and a picnic lunch, and it doesn't take a rocket scientist to figure out that somebody better be paying pretty close attention to all of that too.

What does all of that have to do with how guys and girls are different? Perhaps it's kind of simplistic, but some real connections exist here. You see, God gave men the job of guiding or aiming the family. To be effective, he has to be able to give his total attention to what is downstream and focus all of his abilities on keeping the family safe and secure and headed in the right direction.

Focus is essential for his role. If he takes his eyes off the water for even a few seconds, the canoe can snag, jolt or flip. He must pay attention and lead with his eyes open. So imagine that the husband is sitting in the front of the canoe. His eyes are focused on what is downstream. He is communicating with his wife and sharing information so that

the best path is chosen to keep the family safe.

Women have a different role in our imaginary canoe. It is up to the woman to follow the lead of the man. If we start trying to steer in a different direction or argue with his leadership, we will risk getting sideways in the water, heading under the low tree limbs, or worse. There simply cannot be two leaders in a canoe. One must choose the role of follower, choosing to submit to the leader. Makes sense, right?

Besides, imagine for a moment that a mom and dad are in a canoe with their son and daughter. Lunch is tucked inside as well as is a first-aid kit. The little family starts heading toward rough waters. Where is Dad's focus? Downstream. He's focused on finding the best path and how to get through safely. And Mom? She's focused on everything else. Did the kids put their life vests on correctly? Did they put the lid on the cooler tightly enough? Did they pack everyone's lunch? She has her mind and attention on several different things and people at once. It is hard for her to focus on only one thing.

Perhaps this is a bit of an oversimplification, but there is a basic design truth in this small picture of the family. God, in His immeasurable wisdom, knew that the roles He designed for the family were so important that He even designed male and female brains differently to complement the roles. He actually created our brains to be the best fit for our roles.

Brain Difference #1: Seamless connections or a few narrow paths.

First, did you know that the human brain is divided into two parts, a left side and a right side, called hemispheres? Each of these hemispheres has a different purpose and guides a different part of our thinking process. The left hemisphere is mainly responsible for logical thinking, such as "Step one leads to step two, which leads to step three," etc. We need this part of our brain for logic-based decision making. It helps us take in information about our world, process it, and make choices about how to respond.

The right side of our brain, on the other hand, handles emotions. It is here (not in our hearts) that we feel joy, contentment, anger, sadness, peace, and a whole host of other emotions. This part of our brain separates us from being mere robots. We can, with this right side, factor in how we feel about a situation or a person, which can provide a guide to relationships and decisions.

Although both men and women have these two sides, God designed a key difference between the two genders. Between these two sides in a woman's brain are many, many connectors. These connectors work kind of like train tracks, carrying information from one side of the brain to the other. In fact, in a woman's brain so many of these connectors exist that information between logic and emotion flow freely back and forth. For most women, this makes the shift between the two sides almost automatic and effortless. We may not even be aware of the shift.

Men, on the other hand, have a lot fewer of these connectors in their brains. So they tend to deal with information from only one side at a time: logic or emotion. Men are focused, and most men tend to "live" on the logic side, meaning that is the most natural side for their attention to rest. So because there are fewer connectors, men typically find shifting from one side of their brain to the other more of a challenge than women do.

Think About It
How does that help him in his role?

As the leader of the family, many times a husband must make decisions that impact the whole family. God knew that at times that would be extremely difficult. So He designed man with the ability to examine a decision from both a logical and emotional standpoint without being overwhelmed by both at the same time. In our canoe example, the husband can focus on the logic of which way is best and make his best decision without being as distracted by the emotion of the moment.

Likewise, God designed the woman to uniquely fill her role. She is the one given key responsibility for maintaining the home atmosphere in a loving and nurturing way. To do this well, she needs to be tuned in to the emotional music of her home at all times. She needs to be aware of the tones and moods and how to respond to them in ways that promote a loving home atmosphere. She cannot, though, make those choices without constant contact with her logical brain side. Emotions without connection to logic lead to chaos. God knew that a steady diet of emotions alone would drive women crazy! He knew we needed an even balance of logic along with our strong connection to emotions to nurture our children, our husband, our family and our friends.

Women need the ability to go back and forth between the two sides as if they were one. In the canoe, she needs the ability to listen and respond to her husband's leadings (logic) while she is equally focused on her children's signs of fear, offering them words of comfort and peace (emotions) as they face a challenge together. The man has the lead; the woman is following, yet keenly focused on her key role of nurturing.

Remember how woman was created as the "help counterpart?" God knew that the family would need a balance of roles and strengths. So He gave men the gift of less connected brain sides so that man could lead without being overwhelmed with emotion. He provided man's counterpart, woman, with the ability to have active, instant contact with the family's emotional climate and the ability to call on logic to frame a nurturing reaction in a seamless manner. And although both designs have strengths, both also have limits.

Men, for instance, sometimes find it hard to shift to their emotional sides. They can appear insensitive or uncaring. They must make a more conscious decision to shift to their emotional side in order to nurture and respond to their families. Women, on the other hand, may find it difficult to set emotion aside when necessary to make a decision or handle a problem. We can feel overwhelmed with emotions to the point of not being able to act. This is why women are sometimes accused of being too emotional. We typically cry more easily and can get our feelings hurt more easily.

Yet in a family, when a woman and a man join together bringing each one's strengths and helping each other's weaknesses, a complete-ness results. God's plan: two separate, different puzzle pieces coming together to create a whole. Within this context, He blesses their efforts to add children. Within this completeness, children are best nurtured when fathers are providing loving leadership and mothers are carefully monitoring and nurturing the children as they mature and grow.

Brain Difference #2: One at a time or everything at once.

The second key brain difference in men and women is closely related to this first idea. I've heard it described in many ways, but my favorite description comes from a book by Bill and Pam Farrel, *Men Are Like Waffles – Women Are Like Spaghetti*. The idea here, relating back to the design of our brains, is that men tend to think about one thing at a time in compartments, like the squares of a waffle.

Have you ever tried to talk to a guy about one thing when he was focused on something else? If you have, you might have seen him get frustrated, glaze over, and look kind of dazed or just totally ignore you. He's probably not being rude; his brain is just not wired to swap gears quickly. Men are problem solvers, logical thinkers, focused. They like to figure out the solution to one situation, start to finish. If you interrupt them by trying to talk about something else while they are processing, it's a tremendous challenge for them to hear you and refocus their attention on what you are saying. Don't ask him to tell you what he wants for lunch tomorrow while he's trying to steer the canoe through this gap today – it's not going to happen!

A woman, on the other hand, can simultaneously plan dinner, start a load of laundry, talk on the phone, and play peek-a-boo with her toddler. Have you ever talked on the phone, done homework, listened to the radio, and dreamed about a guy who caught your attention? Easy, right? "Canoe Mom" was following her husband's directions; watching out for the kids; keeping an eye on lunch; and, oh, probably wondering if her hair was frizzing in the humidity. We are, by design, multitaskers.

Think About It

- What do you think would have happened to our canoe family if the husband and wife hadn't fulfilled their roles? What if they had tried to take on each other's roles instead of their own?

- What evidence do you see in God's design of male and female brains that shows His concern for us as we fill our roles on the earth?

- How can a woman use her God-designed brain in her Christian walk whether she is married or not? What about a man?

Recap

So we can see how through our God-designed brains, God has prepared us for the tasks ahead. Men have a greater separation between logic and emotion and can focus in on one task or decision to the exclusion of other distractions, enhancing his leadership role. Women's increased connections enable her to tap both logic and emotion rather seamlessly, enhancing her role as nurturer. Now that we've looked at God's awesome brain design, let's move to some differences that are probably more familiar.

Physical Difference #1: Physical strength and stamina.

Physically, men and women are different, a fact that is clear at first glance. Aside from the obvious difference in sexual organs and body shapes, men generally are stronger, designed with more muscle mass than women. Men can generally "out-muscle" a woman, but women usually have more stamina. It is kind of like the tortoise and hare story.

Read About It
1 Peter 3:7

Think About It

Depending on your Bible version, you may find that the husband is to give "honor to the wife, as to the weaker vessel" (NKJV) or is to live with his wife "in an understanding way, showing honor to the woman as the weaker vessel" (ESV). Why do you think God gave this special note to men here?

The term "manhandle" implies rough or aggressive treatment. Even as little boys, "rough and tumble" play is often the norm. Here, God reminds men to soften their approach when it comes to caring for women.

Physical Difference #2: Roller coasters or light switches.

Physical differences between men and women don't stop with strength. Most girls, by mid-teen years, know about another physical difference as they experience the beginning of a monthly cycle. God created this cycle within us to help us prepare for the days in which we would become pregnant. Along with this cycle, God planted hormones in us that drive both the physical process as well as our emotional responses. When we are ovulating, or releasing an egg from our ovaries, we are generally in a better mood and feel happier. As we move toward our periods, though – ugh! We tend to feel more tired and depressed and, let's face it, downright crabby.

But your Creator knew that this cycle of emotions is important in helping us prepare physically to have children. The upward side of the cycle happens when we are most likely to become pregnant. So a woman is most interested in being with her husband sexually when she is most likely to become pregnant. However, as she moves forward through her cycle before and during her period, she is less interested in sex, giving her body time to cleanse and reset for the next egg to be released. So a woman's emotional and physical cycle looks a bit like a roller coaster with ups and downs that cycle back and forth.

The **Girls**

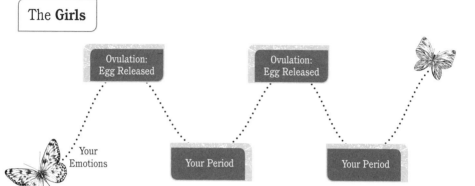

Men, however, don't experience this kind of cycle. When guys go through puberty and their sexual hormones turn on, they essentially stay on – steadily – for most of their lives. They are more like light switches. Once that "switch" in their bodies gets turned on, it stays on. So their desire and interest in sex is fairly consistent and constant. God prepared men to be ready for the time in which their wives' bodies could best respond. By having a steady sex drive, a husband can respond to his wife's changing interests and needs.

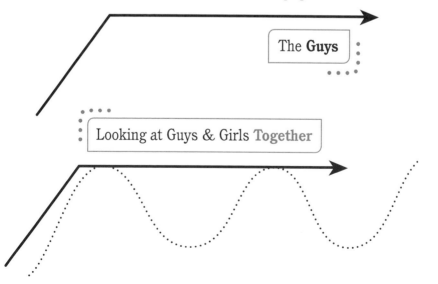

Read About It
Genesis 1:28

Think About It

- God clearly intended children to be created within the context of a husband/wife relationship. How does His design of our physical cycles help fulfill that design?

- What does this say to guys and girls about when temptation to sin sexually is hardest?

For guys, temptation is fairly constant, requiring them to always be on guard. Girls, on the other hand, tend to find that their sexual interests and temptations intensify or decrease as they go through the ups and downs of their monthly cycles. This does mean, however, that girls tend to be most vulnerable to temptation when they are most likely to become pregnant.

Physical Difference #3: Touch or sight.

One more key difference in this area of sexual attraction is important to consider. It is important for us as women (and the guys too) to understand that what tends to attract a woman to a man is not the same as what attracts a man to a woman. Guys tend to be attracted by what they see, such as how a woman looks, how she is dressed, how she moves. Women, on the other hand, tend to be more attracted by touch.

Now, that doesn't mean that a woman won't notice a good looking guy or that a guy doesn't appreciate a tender hug. However, it does mean that how they each see and experience the world is different. A guy's attraction to a girl is much more influenced by what he sees. This is why men can so easily become addicted to pornography. Although women can have trouble in this area as well, it is much more of a temptation to men. God created them to be attracted by sight. Satan will use any means he can to turn God's good design to evil.

A girl, though, is much more sensitive to touch than a guy. We've all seen it, haven't we? Some guy barely brushes against some girl in the hall at school, and she just goes to pieces: "He touched me! Did you see that? I'll never wash this sweater again!" And she can go on for days on that slightest little touch that he probably didn't even notice. God designed us to be aroused differently.

And Satan is busy here, too. Satan has taught some guys how to abuse that godly design to manipulate a girl's attention. Have you seen a guy who can suddenly become all "huggy" and tender to some girl when all he really has in mind is getting his own selfish desires met? Because sex involves affection, some women will compromise their bodies sexually to get the affection (touch) they crave. You can see it if you're standing back watching. Be careful though! If you are the one getting the affection, it can easily blind you to what is happening.

Think About It

- Think, again, about the roles God gave us. Why do you think God designed a man's eyes to be so important to him and touch to be so important for a woman?

- How can these desires work for good?

- How can Satan use them for evil?

Summing It Up

God was not haphazard in His design. He was purposeful, and as He said in Genesis, His results were "very good" (1:31). He knew what roles we each would be taking in the family, and He designed us to fit perfectly into those roles. Granted, we are human, and we mess up, but His design was intended to give us the hope and future that He has in store for all of us.

We will look at more differences between guys and girls in the next lesson. Then, we will think about how to aim the many gifts God has given us in His rich design toward having the life He wants for His precious daughters.

Talk About It

1. What in this chapter surprised you the most?

2. What are some examples you see in the world of these designs being misused?

3. How can we use our design as women to honor God whether married or unmarried?

Pray About It

Lord, Your awesome design through Your immeasurable wisdom continues to amaze us. Help us see, as we go through this week, the evidence of Your design. Teach us to thank You when we see You in our daily lives, for we know You designed us in love.

Recommended Reading

Men Are Like Waffles, Women Are Like Spaghetti by Bill Farrel and Pam Farrel (Eugene: Harvest House, 2007). Using a healthy sprinkling of humor, the Farrels explain how a man is more like a waffle, placing each element of his life in a separate box, while a woman is more like spaghetti with everything in her life intermingled. The book provides good guidance for married couples as well as for male/female interactions in other settings.

Chapter 7

Guys and Girls Are Different, Part Two

Recap

The previous chapter focused on some key differences in the way in which God designed male and female bodies in keeping with their respective roles. Brain development, physical strength and stamina, and hormones are a few examples of His amazing wisdom. This chapter will continue this exploration, focusing on emotional differences.

Opening Reflections

A dear friend of mine had a crush on an older guy for several years. He lived in another town and had really never paid her any attention until he showed up on her doorstep one day. He was passing through town and found out where she lived. They went out that evening, ending the time with some rather passionate kissing in the car before she went inside. He declared his love for her and said he wanted to marry her. She immediately shared her elation with her family and a few close friends.

A few weeks later, he married someone else. As you can imagine, her emotional high from before immediately plummeted to an incredible low. This illustrates one important point about our emotions. There is a difference between having our emotional needs met temporarily versus long-term. What happens over time makes the difference.

Starting Point

What would the world be like without any emotion? What would you miss?

God designed us as emotional beings, and He, too, is emotional. While we won't take time for this right now, on your own explore the emotions of God. See what the Bible says about what God feels and why. It is an interesting study all by itself.

But for today, we are going to explore another difference in guys and girls that relates to emotions. Remember that both men and women have a right side of the brain, which focuses on emotions. And because of that, we each, male and female, have emotional needs. But these needs tend to be different, in keeping with God's awesome design.

Take a look at the list below. It is a simple list of six emotional needs in alphabetical order – needs that we all have, male and female.[1] I don't want to do without any of them. Do you?

(1) Affection (sharing hugs, smiles, friendly affection with another person).

(2) Communication (talking openly to another person).

(3) Respect from others (feeling like other people respect or look up to me).

(4) Safety and security (feeling like I am in a safe and secure setting).

(5) Self-respect (feeling good about myself).

(6) Sense of accomplishment (feeling like I have done something of value or importance).

Although we all have these six needs, when asked to list them in order of importance, men and women usually rank them differently. Although there are a lot of differences between individuals and how they view this list, three of these usually make the guys' top three list and three usually rise to the top of girls' lists. Can you guess which ones go to which lists?

Think About It

Take a minute to jot down your answers, and note which three would be at the top of your own personal list.

Think about it from the perspective of the roles God designed. A leader needs all six of these. However, without the respect of those he is leading, he is in big trouble. And a leader must have a drive to accomplish goals for both himself and for the ones he leads; otherwise, how would he decide where to lead? Which way do you head if you have no real desire to reach a goal or accomplish anything? And finally, without self-respect, a man cannot be a very effective leader. If he does not feel good about himself, how can he encourage others to follow him?

And the woman, the nurturer, can be successful only if she is comfortable talking openly with those whom she is nurturing. She must also be comfortable holding and rocking her children, showing affection to her husband, and kissing "boo-boos" when her child hurts. Yet to do all of this, she must feel safe and secure. Otherwise, she is likely to pull in physically or emotionally to protect herself, limiting her ability to reach out to the very ones who need her.

Read About It
Ephesians 5:23-33

Think About It
Where, in these verses, do you see God hinting or sometimes directly saying what men and women's emotional needs are?

These six emotional needs are all very important and can be very strong motivators in our lives. When these needs are met appropriately, we feel good inside. But when we get off-track in seeking them, we can create quite a mess! We can easily get sidetracked chasing an emotional need if we don't keep an eye on the clock. By that I mean for true emotional needs to be met, they have to be secure over time. Let me explain that by telling you a story.

It starts simply: Boy meets girl. Boy, let's call him "Bob," meets girl, let's call her "Sue." They could be at school, at a party, or at work. That doesn't much matter. But for now, let's say they meet at a party. Bob sees her right off and is interested. (Remember, guys are most attracted by sight.) He walks over to introduce himself and holds out his hand, which she accepts in a brief but gentle shake. ("He touched me!" Her heart flutters a bit!) They begin seeing each other from time to time, and each time, the talk and the touches get more intimate.

Over time – and it usually does take time – they get more and more intimate to the point that one night, while no one else is around, they go all the way to having sex together.

Now, let's freeze-frame this story for a minute. Picture them together, cuddled up. She is thinking, "Ahh, how wonderfully **affectionate** he is. I can **talk** to him about anything, and I feel so **safe** in his arms right now. This is wonderful!" Sounds like her emotional needs are met, right? Security? Affection? Communication? All there. But wait – the story doesn't end there. We aren't to the clock yet. Hold that thought.

Bob is smiling satisfactorily with his arms around his "prize." He has **accomplished** something. He feels good about himself **(self-respect)**. "I must be pretty special for her to have given herself to me. Wait till I tell the guys tomorrow. They will really think I'm something!" **(respect from others)**. (Yes, girls, they will talk.) His needs met?

Don't forget about the clock.

Let's unfreeze the moment and let the clock tick. It is a few days later now. Bob walks into the building a bit late and in a hurry. He sees Sue at a distance and is immediately seething. Why? She is standing next to another guy (we'll call him Jack), all smiles and such, and "Look at what she is wearing!" Bob thinks. (Sight is important to a guy, and she is wearing a skirt that is a little too short and a blouse that is a little too low.)

He is sure this other guy is noticing that too, and he is angry. But he is also late, so there's no time to talk right now. He sulks over to his locker and begins angrily flinging books in. Jan, his locker neighbor, walks up and sees his obvious unsettledness. She quietly asks him if he is okay. He sighs: "Yeah, I'm just mad at my girlfriend. Thanks for asking. You're a good friend." And he gives her a quick hug.

Guess who saw him give Jan a hug. You guessed it. Now Sue is upset! (Touch is important to a girl.) But there's no time now, so she turns and walks briskly off the other way before he sees her looking in his direction.

The clock keeps ticking. A couple of hours pass, and now it is lunchtime. Bob and Sue usually enjoy a few minutes together over lunch, but today is different. She is already seated at a table surrounded by her girlfriends when he walks in. Guess what they are talking about. She is weeping, and they are consoling. (Female nurturers at work.) He walks up and begins to confront her:

"I **saw** [important word] you this morning flirting with Jack! What was that all about? I thought you were my girl? And why are you dressed like that? You've got every guy here **staring** at you!"

"What was I doing?" she fires back. "What about you? I saw you with your **arms** all over Jan! [Touch is powerful! Sue knows it.] I thought your **arms** were for me?"

Do you hear her need to feel safe and secure?

And the exchange goes on ... and gets uglier ... and louder ... finally ending with Sue and her friends running off to the bathroom while Bob stalks away in anger. Now maybe they work this disagreement out; maybe they don't. The bottom line is that, by far, the majority of couples who have sex before marriage do not stay together long-term. Sooner or later, they break up, leaving a trail of hurt and disappointment.

And the clock ticks further. Two months have passed now, and Sue just discovered she is eight weeks pregnant. Now what? Is she finding **affection** from Bob? How do you think the **communication** is going? If they are talking at all, it probably isn't very fulfilling. And what about feeling **safe** and **secure**? She is probably feeling anything BUT that right now.

And Bob? Feeling good about himself or **self respect**? Doubtful. He's probably feeling pretty low. **Respect of others?** He most likely has to "duck and cover" any time one of her friends comes near. Not fun! And what about his sense of **accomplishment**? Where is his "prize" now?

You see, Satan is really good at making us think we are getting our emotional needs met. But what he is really doing is setting up a cheap alternative to cheat us out of the real thing. It's no different than setting cheese in a mouse trap. Poor little guy thinks he will get his needs met. Looks good; must be good. Right up until that snap. Then he has fallen for a trap that is at least painful and, at worst, deadly.

Now just in case you missed it, the point about the clock is this: Emotional needs can truly be met only out of genuine love, that *agape* love we discussed several lessons ago that says, "I choose what is best for you **over time**," not just what feels good for the moment. Stepping out of God's will is never going to be what is best for any of us over time. So if a friend, a boyfriend, or whoever is trying to get you to move in a direction other than what God has designed, you can be sure it is not love. Love seeks what is best over time.

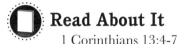

Read About It
1 Corinthians 13:4-7

(Note that the word translated "love" or "charity" in this passage is *agape* in the Greek.)

Think About It
What words do you read in this passage that tell you love keeps an eye on what is best over time?

Summing It Up
It is absolutely amazing to me how God formed us with every tiny detail aimed toward what was best for us. Can't you see His love for His children in how He put us together? So amazing! From our physical to our mental and even to our emotional make-up, He has a plan.

Talk About It
1. Have you seen any "Bob and Sue" relationships? What kind of heartache followed? How did others react to them?

2. What commercials have you seen that distract us from the idea of the clock?

3. Why is it so easy to forget about what is best in the long run?

4. Can we have our emotional needs filled properly without being married? If so, how?

5. In what ways does God fill our top three emotional needs as women?

6. How does He fill the top three emotional needs of men?

Pray About It
Thank You, precious Father, for creating us to experience emotion in our world. Thank You that we are not mere robots without the ability to love, laugh and enjoy so much that You have set before us. Yet, Lord, we recognize that Satan would love nothing more than to destroy everything that You have created. Teach us to guard our hearts and to be watchful for the hearts of those around us. Help us to forever remember the importance

of thinking about our decisions over time. And dear Father, help us to seek You for our emotional needs, knowing that You, our Father, know better than anyone else how to satisfy our needs. Thank You, Father.

Recommended Reading

• *Captivating: Unveiling the Mystery of a Woman's Soul* by John Eldredge and Stasi Eldredge (Nashville: Thomas Nelson, 2011). The counterpart to *Wild at Heart*, *Captivating* talks about the heart of a woman. Reading both books provides great insight into the differences between how men and women think.

• *For Women Only: What You Need to Know About the Inner Lives of Men* by Shaunti Christine Feldhahn (Sisters: Multnomah, 2004). This is a short, refreshing read about the extremely different ways that men and women's minds work and how men (try to) understand women. It is very illuminating to read about the male mind in girl language and, in so doing, to learn how to communicate better with your significant other.

• *His Needs, Her Needs: Building an Affair-Proof Marriage*, revised and expanded edition, by Willard F. Harley (Grand Rapids: Revell, 2011). This book was written to married couples but says volumes about the emotional differences in men and women.

• *Wild at Heart: Discovering the Secret of a Man's Soul* by John Eldredge (Nashville: Thomas Nelson, 2001). Eldredge uses real-life stories and examples from popular movies to help explain the workings of a man's heart.

Chapter 8

Connected

Opening Reflections

When I decided to pursue a master's degree, a key consideration for me was a program that did not require a thesis. To me, the idea of having to write a document of that magnitude on my own was unthinkable. Yet as I neared the end of my academic studies, circumstances in my family were such that I really needed to select the thesis route to finishing instead of the practicum route I had anticipated. I was so close to finishing, but now this almost insurmountable obstacle loomed in my future.

Starting Point

Imagine your boss or teacher gives you a massive, important assignment. It is vital, as in it will make or break your company or affect your ability to graduate. How do you feel?

It can sometimes feel like we are carrying the weight of the world on our shoulders. We have so much to do – so many deadlines and so much crammed into our schedules – and now, this boss or teacher has put a huge responsibility in our laps. "This is too hard! It's too much! I can't handle it!"

But what if, along with the responsibility, this boss/teacher says: "I know this is a really tough assignment, but I'm going to give you everything you need to get the job done. Need guidance? Got it! Need people to help? Got it! Resources? They are yours! In fact, I'm going to go so far to ensure your success that I am going to provide you with a magic pill that will physically help you get the work done"? (No, we aren't talking about drug abuse; this is a pretend magic pill just for the illustration.) Now, how do you feel about this task? More hopeful? Encouraged? Relieved?

 Read About It
2 Peter 1:2-4

 Think About It
What has Jesus given to us? What is the significance of Peter's stating that we have all things we need for both life and godliness?

We've been given a task of major importance: to protect and preserve marriage and families. But God didn't dump this responsibility in our laps and walk away leaving us to bear it alone. Instead, He wanted us to be so capable of success that He has provided all that we need to make it happen. He has given us instructions through His Word and people to help through the church. And remember the magic pill? Well, there is no pill; however, He has given us something even better. It is absolutely amazing!

Our bodies depend on many different naturally occurring chemicals that regulate a vast number of different functions. Did you know God actually placed certain chemicals in your body designed to help you preserve your family? It is true! And it is an incredible faith-building phenomenon. Although there are lots of pieces to this God-created design, two of them are particularly relevant to this discussion: One is primarily active in females, and one, in males.

Girls' Brain Glue

Girls have a chemical that is released in their brains called **oxytocin**.[1] It is released at four specific times in a woman's life:

(1) When she is experiencing meaningful and intimate touching with another person.
(2) During sexual intercourse.

(3) During labor and delivery.

(4) When breast-feeding her baby.

Oxytocin's job is to act like glue, bonding or connecting a woman to the person she is with at the time.

Think About It

Look again at the moments when oxytocin is released. What connection do you see among these circumstances?

Assuming that a woman is living within God's boundaries for the family, who are the people to which this woman will feel connected? Her husband (intimate touch and sexual intercourse) and her children (childbirth and nursing). In this way, God has equipped a woman to feel connected to her family. This chemical actually leads to feelings of connection. Is that not amazing?

Assume for a moment that a woman does not have sex or participate in intimate touching with anyone before she is married. Then, imagine that she marries and, over the next few years, has two children. She is now experiencing the release of oxytocin in her body on a regular basis, all of which reinforces the connection she feels for her husband and children. Imagine, next, that she has to be away from her family for a time – a week or so. Whom does she miss? To whom is she eager to return? Her family! This is, in part, the work of oxytocin.

Let me describe it another way. Humans are not the only female mammals that experience the release of oxytocin in their bodies. Many in the animal kingdom experience the release of this chemical at least during childbirth to reinforce the mother's instinct to care for her young. My family witnessed this firsthand when our 18-month-old dachshund, Sara, gave birth to her first litter of puppies.

Sara is absolutely the most outgoing, fun-loving, never-met-a-stranger dog I have ever seen. In fact, that is why we picked her as a puppy. We took our 3-year-old male dog, Oscar, along to help select her. At the time, her owner had two puppies left. The little blonde female was beautiful and immediately caught my attention. The owner also had a sweet little solid black female. We set Oscar and the two puppies in the back of a pickup truck to see how the little ones would respond to him. The blonde immediately ran under a toolbox and hid while the little black one trotted up to him, stood on her back legs, and playfully whacked him across the nose, inviting him to play. Guess which one is our Sara. Yep, Sara is solid black.

From the moment we brought her home, the two dogs have been inseparable best friends. They play together, sleep in one big bed together, and stay virtually side by side all day. That was, until the puppies were born. With a healthy dose of oxytocin in little mama's body, her disposition took an immediate stark change. No one was welcome in her baby turf except for my husband and me. And we were tolerated only for occasional, brief visits – and we didn't dare pick up the babies!

Oscar, though, became the enemy. She would not let him within 2 feet of the babies without making it *very* clear that he was not welcome! And with good reason. You see, he did not have the oxytocin experience of childbirth. Even though he was the dad, he clearly didn't feel the same connection to the little pups. In those first two weeks, the pups looked more like moles than baby dogs, and Oscar's experience with moles was not overly friendly, especially for the mole. Even as the puppies began to grow and look like puppies, Sara fiercely protected them. When Oscar would approach the box that was their "home," she would run over and position her body across the babies and peer at him, sometimes growling until he moved on. It wasn't until after she quit nursing them that we saw her returning to a more comfortable relationship with the others around her.

Now dogs don't typically choose a mate for life nor do they typically remain with their pups for life. And they lack the brain development that enhances the effect of this chemical as in the human brain. But even with those modifications, this typically sweet little gal would have eaten a bear alive to protect her babies. That's oxytocin at its best.

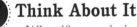 ## Think About It

What if oxytocin is released, connecting a girl to someone who is not her husband?

Let's say, for example, a girl is physically involved (remember it only has to be intimate touching, not necessarily sexual intercourse) with some guy she's been dating. If you've ever watched daytime talk shows, you've seen this story. Picture on the stage seated next to the program host this woman who is reasonably attractive, holds down a decent job, but is living with this guy sitting on her other side. This guy can't hold a job for more than a week or two at a time and doesn't look like he has bothered to shave or bathe in who knows how long. He cheats on her at least once a week and beats her up frequently. The host, trying to counsel the woman, urges her to leave him. But the woman's response? "I can't leave him because I _____ _____."

Do you know how she ends the sentence? Right. "I can't leave him because I *love him.*" This is what oxytocin does. In the right situation, in the family, it helps to bond a woman to her husband and her children. However, applied in the wrong situation, it makes a woman feel trapped in what she knows isn't right. You probably know of girls who keep breaking up and making up with some guy who is *clearly* not good for her. You ask her why she keeps going back, but she doesn't seem to know: "I don't know. I just can't stop thinking about him."

This is a powerful chemical. Breaking its connections is hard even when the individuals recognize the need to break up. And what about the women who move from one sexual relationship to another – dating, touching intimately, breaking up, only to repeat the cycle again and again? What happens to all of those connections? Did you know that the brain actually begins to adapt to this misuse? The brain actually learns to associate those feelings of connection with breaking up, the exact opposite of what God intended.

Our brains, on the unconscious level, actually change with our experiences and our behavior patterns. To illustrate, grab a piece of clear packing tape. You know, the really sticky kind. Stick it on your bare arm really snuggly. Now, rip it off really fast. How was that? Painful? Did it leave some of you attached to the tape? Probably! But do it again. Take that same piece of tape and stick it back on your arm. Jerk it off again. Still hurts, right? But maybe not quite so badly. Try reusing the sticky tape a dozen or so times and chances are it won't stick at all anymore. Does that mean it was faulty to begin with? No, of course not. It was quite able to do what it was designed to do until it was misused. Only then did it fail in its purpose.

So does all of this mean that if a woman saves all of the oxytocin-releasing experiences of her life until after she is married that she will live "happily ever after"? No. Oxytocin is only one tool God places within you to help you with this task. It alone cannot preserve a marriage. But it is a powerful "glue" to help in the process.

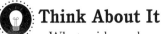

Think About It
- What evidence have you seen of oxytocin at work?

- Have you known of women who protected this gift? Have you known women who didn't? What were some of the results with both?

- How does knowing God cared enough about you and your family to equip you in this way make you feel?

Guys' Brain Glue

Now, let's look at the guys' side of the story. Their main brain chemical aid is **vasopressin**. It works in very similar ways in a man's body as oxytocin does in a woman's. Both are intended to create a sense of bonding through physical intimacy or touching. So as a man spends time touching his wife intimately, vasopressin is released, which serves as his "brain glue," attaching him to her.

One of the unique characteristics of this chemical, though, is that it actually creates very detailed visual images that are stored in a man's brain. Think of it like a huge scrapbook of times when he has enjoyed being with his wife intimately and sexually. (Remember how guys are attracted by sight? A perfect fit!) So let's imagine that this man has been faithfully married to his wife and had no previous intimacy with any other women. His "photo album" is full of pictures only of her. Now, imagine he has to be away from her for a week or so. Who is he thinking about? Who is he picturing in his mind? Who is he eager to get home to? His wife, of course!

But like oxytocin, vasopressin can be misused and abused. Imagine now a different situation where a guy has been physically intimate with many different women. He has his brain-based picture album full of snapshots of lots of women. Then he finds the woman he wants to marry and remain faithful to for the rest of his life. Yet when he comes to her on their wedding night, the photo album in his head pops open and starts flashing pictures of the other women all through his brain.

Think About It
What do you think that will do to this young couple? What struggles will they face?

Like oxytocin, vasopressin is intended to be a brain-bonding agent. Like oxytocin, if it is misused, it fails to provide its intended gluing ability. Remember the tape? The same is true for men. If they make and break intimate relationships again and again, the bonding affect of vasopressin becomes ineffective.

Think About It

- What are some challenges guys might face in protecting this chemical bond?

- What do you think it would be like to be married to a man who has protected this bond? What would it be like if he hasn't?

- How does it make you feel to know God cared enough about you and your family to equip men in this way?

Now, let's spend a few minutes on the "what ifs" that always surface from this discussion when I share this face to face: "What if I've already been physically intimate or had sex with someone who I am not married to? Am I just doomed to be 'messed up' from my misuse of these chemicals?" Thanks be to God, the answer is no. But it is a process – sometimes a long process. Fortunately, the effects of these chemicals tend to lessen over time if not reinforced.

Let's go back to the example of our little dog Sara. Although this is not an exact mirror of the human experience, we could easily see the effects of oxytocin wearing off with her as she weaned her babies. Now humans, of course, have lots of different reasons for connecting to people around them. But for Sara, her simply designed dog brain was just reacting to this chemical. So we could clearly observe the changes in her as she no longer had the chemical coursing through her veins from nursing.

The "cure" to misuse of these chemicals is time. If you have been sexually active with someone who is not your spouse (which includes intimate touching, not just intercourse), the answer to getting back on track is **stop**. But let's be honest here: Stopping is tough. Really tough. It is going to take a strong conviction in your left brain (logic side) to overpower the emotional connection that is powerfully established within you. Recognize it for what it is, and remind yourself that what you are doing is cleansing your brain and preparing it for that time when the bond is appropriate: within marriage.

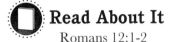
Read About It
Romans 12:1-2

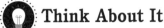
Think About It

- How will protecting these chemicals in our bodies be different from what the world promotes?

- How, in this situation, will renewing our minds prove what is good about God's will for us?

Finally, to married women, I want to remind you of what you have been given. Remember from earlier lessons that males have a stronger, more consistent sex drive than women typically do. Part of the responsibility you have as a godly wife is to protect your family and, particularly, your husband in this matter. That means you have a responsibility to be very sensitive to his needs in this area and be responsive so that he is not tempted to add other women's pictures to his album. Although you cannot control his choices, you can ensure that you are doing your best to meet his needs. Don't neglect this important bond between the two of you.

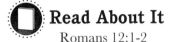
Read About It
1 Corinthians 7:1-5

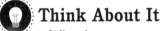
Think About It

- What is one reason that Paul gave for choosing marriage? What does that say about the power of our God-given sexual desires?

- Why, in light of what we have discussed in this section, do you think God took the time to lay clear expectations that a wife and husband meet each other's needs sexually?

Summing It Up

God has given us everything that pertains to life and godliness (2 Peter 1:3) right down to the very intricate design of the chemicals flowing through our bodies. He wants us to be successful in living this life to its fullest. But like nearly everything in His world, when we misuse it, the result is pain and destruction. God knew this would happen. This love-spirit-truth God knew the pain we would experience if we chose to give our bodies away to those who were not our mates. But He also knew the intense joy that could be experienced in a dedicated, loving family, and He provided an ample supply of "brain glue" to help us along the way. So His warnings guiding us away from sex outside of marriage are not intended to keep us from having fun. Instead, He is inviting us to a joy that can only be experienced when we align our bodies' desires with His will.

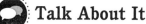

Talk About It

1. What does this discussion do for your faith?

2. What are some practical guidelines that would help an unmarried man or woman protect the gift of these chemicals until he or she is married?

3. What are some practical guidelines that would help a married man or woman protect these gifts?

Pray About It

Our dear loving Maker, thank You so much for providing what we need in both this life and in the one to come. We are so grateful for Your loving design, which helps us cling to our families in a world that rejects the bonds You designed. Help us, as women, to honor and protect this gift by preserving it within marriage. Give us wisdom to see Satan's lies and give us strength to choose what is right. Thank You, Lord, for Your unfailing love.

Recommended Reading

Hooked: New Science on How Casual Sex Is Affecting Our Children by Joe S. McIlhaney and Freda McKissic Bush (Chicago: Northfield Pub., 2008). By far, the best book I have ever read on how these chemicals work in our brains is *Hooked*. Dr. Joe McIlhaney describes the chemical reactions and results in a clear, nontechnical manner that can be easily understood. Although he writes from a medical perspective, the principles he discloses directly align with God's principles.

Chapter 9

Protected

Opening Reflections

A number of years ago, a friend of mine became extremely worried about her husband. He had become distant and moody, hardly coming near her for any reason at all. When he was around, he was an absolute grouch. She began to worry that he was sick or dying or, worse, having an affair. Weeks went by with his unrelenting emotional wall intact. She felt crushed and abandoned. One day, though, he came in and pulled her into his embrace. He began to cry as he shared with her that he had been waiting on results from medical tests that he was afraid to share with her. Because of some premarital sexual partners, he had been terrified to learn that he could have been exposed to HIV, the virus that causes AIDS. Just a few years into their marriage, a positive test result would mean that he had very likely delivered a death sentence to himself, his young wife, and their baby boy. The waiting was excruciating.

Starting Point

Imagine that a terrible, life-threatening disease was sweeping across the nation. How would you respond?

None of us like being sick, especially really sick. Because of that, I imagine that most of us would get pretty concerned about an epidemic. If that happened in my lifetime, I'd be listening to the news, reading the paper, and looking on the Internet to learn what I needed to do to protect myself and my family. I would be choosing my sources very carefully though because you can find all kinds of nutty advice from the wrong sources. I'd be looking for the most reliable sources I could find, wouldn't you?

Here's a short trivia quiz, and I'm even providing the answers in the box above. When do you think medical professionals began to really stress the following medical advice?

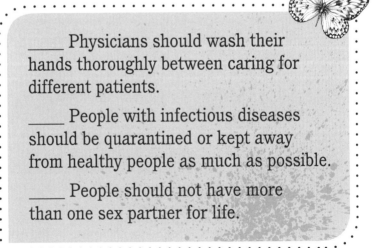

_____ Physicians should wash their hands thoroughly between caring for different patients.

_____ People with infectious diseases should be quarantined or kept away from healthy people as much as possible.

_____ People should not have more than one sex partner for life.

Here's the order of the dates: 1840s, 1340s, 1980s. How did you do? Did any of these surprise you? By now, we are all pretty familiar with these health practices and probably almost take some of them for granted. However, it hasn't always been so. It took the human race a long time to figure out on their own some very basic health practices.

Read About It

- Exodus 15:26
- Deuteronomy 7:12-16

Think About It

- To whom were these verses written?

- What is the promise?

- What is the condition (see Exodus 15:26; Deuteronomy 7:12)?

Here is the setting: God had just delivered the Israelites from Egyptian bondage under the human leadership of Moses. They were moving toward the Promised Land. At this time, God made this promise, saying that He would protect them from the diseases they saw in the land of Egypt *if* they would follow His commands. Was He offering some miraculous protection here in return for obedience? Perhaps. But He was also offering them some guidance that was designed to provide natural protection.

Literally thousands of years before modern science understood the importance of these practices, God gave the Israelites clear, medically sound instructions on all of the practices listed in the quiz above and many, many other common health practices. The guidance to the Israelites was full of very specific rules on cleanliness; care of sick individuals; disposing of deceased bodies; cooking and handling of meat; and even clear, cutting-edge guidance on safe sex practices.

Think About It

- What do you think the Israelites thought about all the rules they were given? (Keep in mind that these were *not* the normal practices of the day.)

- Is it easier to follow directions when you understand the importance or when you just trust the source? Which requires more faith?

- Do you sometimes struggle with following God's commands because you don't understand why they are important? Why? How do we grow beyond this response?

With a clear reminder in place that God will always lead us in the path that is best, let's focus on how this fits with our discussion of sexual purity in today's world. First, another little puzzle: What is the difference between a VD, STD and STI? Have you heard all of these terms? Probably most people today have at least heard the acronym STD, which stands for "sexually transmitted disease" or any disease that can be transmitted or "caught" by having sex with someone who has the disease. What, then, is a VD? VD is an acronym for "venereal disease," which is what STDs were called just a few decades ago. STI – the newest term, short for "sexually transmitted infection" – has recently been introduced as the overarching term for these diseases.

Why the switch from "disease" to "infection"? Some people think "disease" is too scary a word. So there is a push to call these diseases "infections" instead. We'll talk about them a bit, and you decide which term you think is better. For now, though, just understand that whether people talk about VDs, STDs or STIs, they are really talking about the same set of diseases.

Another quick note for context is important to insert here. According to the Centers for Disease Control, although young people ages 15 to 24 make up only 25 percent of the sexually active population in the U.S., this age group makes up nearly half of new STD-diagnosed patients each year. [1] That means that young adults are at the greatest risk for infection than any other age group in the U.S. Keep this in mind as we think through this issue.

Another significant fact to insert here relates to the change in the number of STDs that now cause a threat. Back in the 1960s, only two major sexually transmitted diseases were significant threats: syphilis and gonorrhea. Both were caused by different kinds of bacteria but were easily treatable with penicillin or some other type of antibiotic. Guess how many major STDs there are today. More than 20! [2] That means in just 50 years, there are more than 10 times the number of STDs. That is a significant increase. Among these 20-plus are some caused by bacteria and some by viruses. Do you know the major difference between a bacterial infection and a viral infection? In general, bacterial infections can be treated with antibiotics, but viral infections cannot. That means for some of the diseases we face in our world today, there is no cure.

We aren't going to take time here to talk about all 20-plus of the STDs that are a significant threat to us right now, but I do want you to know a bit about the eight most prevalent threats. Here's the list sorted by which are caused by bacteria and which are caused by viruses:

Bacteria	Virus
Chlamydia	Hepatitis B
Gonorrhea	Hepatitis C
Syphilis	Herpes
	Human Immunodeficiency Virus (HIV)
	Human Papillomavirus (HPV)

Bacterial Diseases

Let's start on the bacteria side. **Chlamydia** and **gonorrhea** are both bacterial infections that can get into the sexual organs of a man or a woman. Once inside, both diseases can cause pelvic inflammatory disease (PID) in women. [3] As the infection moves up into a woman's sexual organs, scar tissue is formed inside. That can be very dangerous. Between a woman's ovaries (where her eggs are released each month) and her uterus (where a baby grows if she is pregnant) is a tiny tube called a fallopian tube. This tiny tube's job is to carry the egg to the uterus once a month. If the egg is fertilized with a man's sperm, the egg will stay in the uterus and a baby will grow there. If not, the egg will go on out of her body, and a couple of weeks later, she will have her period to prepare for the next egg.

The danger if the woman gets one of these infections is that the infection can move into the tiny tubes and grow scar tissue. The scar tissue can start closing off the tiny tube and at some point, if not treated, can close the tube off completely. If that happens, the woman will not be able to have a baby, because the egg will not be able to move to the uterus. But before the tube closes completely, a very dangerous thing can happen. You see the tube may begin to close, trapping the egg in the tube, but a man's sperm is much, much smaller than the egg. So the sperm may be able to get through the tube even after the egg is trapped. If that happens, the sperm can get to the egg, and the woman can become pregnant.

However, since the tube is too small for the egg to travel back to the uterus now, where it is supposed to attach and grow, it is trapped in the tube. This is called an ectopic pregnancy. The problem is that the tube is not made to stretch and grow with the baby as the uterus is. In fact, it cannot stretch much at all. At some point when the baby begins to grow, the tube will burst. If the woman does not receive immediate emergency care, she can quickly bleed to death.

Syphilis, another bacterial infection, is different. Although it too is curable with antibiotics, the problem with it is that most people don't recognize the symptoms until it has done its damage. Syphilis starts as a small sore that doesn't even hurt, and it goes away on its own. In the second stage, syphilis causes a rash that usually doesn't itch, and it also goes away on its own. The third stage, however, attacks the brain, heart and nervous system. Although syphilis is treatable, once damage is done it cannot be reversed. [4]

For all of the bacterial STDs, one added concern is that these diseases are becoming resistant to antibiotics. That means that some of the antibiotics that worked in the past to cure them aren't working as effectively now. That means scientists are struggling to find more and more antibiotics to combat these dangerous diseases. Adding to the difficulty is the fact that many people who are infected with an STD of any kind don't know they are infected, so these STDs can exist and do their damage without any outward symptoms. Keep this detail in mind as we talk further.

Viral Diseases

Although all of the bacterial STDs are huge concerns, the viral STDs are even worse. First, let me remind you that because they are viruses, antibiotics do not work to cure them. Once someone gets a viral STD, he may be dealing with it for the rest of his life. Let's take a quick look at what that would mean for the top five viral STDs.

First, **hepatitis B** and **C** both can be transmitted through sexual activity as well as through contact with blood (such as when drug users share the same needle). Both of these viruses attack the liver and can lead to liver failure. [5] **Herpes**, next on our list, causes very painful sores that will break out in the genital areas. These sores will come and go throughout a person's life because herpes is one of those diseases that will not go away. Even if an infected person doesn't have sores right now, he or she can still pass the disease on to someone else. So a person can *look* okay, but not *be* okay. Herpes also leads to increased cancer risks as well as an increased risk of other STDs through the sores. [6]

Human immunodeficiency virus, or HIV, is the virus that causes AIDS. Basically, if you get HIV, you get AIDS. If you get AIDS, you die. Fortunately, discoveries in medicine are helping to keep someone with AIDS alive longer, but ultimately, it is still a fatal, painful disease. And many of the other STDs are linked to increased chances of being infected with HIV. [7]

Last on our virus list is **human papillomavirus** or HPV for short. When I first started talking to teens and young adults about these topics just a few years ago, only about one in 50 teens had ever heard of HPV. Now that is changing some with the discovery of an immunization against the disease. HPV causes two times more deaths in women than HIV/AIDS because HPV causes a vast majority of cervical cancer cases.

Adding to that concern, HPV also can cause genital warts that form in the genital areas of men or women. These are very painful and sometimes have to be removed by surgery or cauterization (burning them off). And because HPV is a virus, the warts can come back again and again and again. Fortunately, immunizations for HPV and hepatitis B and C are helping to curb the number of cases of these deadly diseases, but the risks still exist. [8]

Think About It

- How many of these eight STDs had you heard about?

- If many people who have STDs don't know it, what concerns does that raise?

Convinced that you don't want to deal with having one of these STDs in your life? I hope you said, "Yes!" The good news is that while all eight of these are very serious illnesses with very serious consequences, they are also very preventable.

So here's a puzzle for you. Below is a picture of what we will call the "Chain of Infection." It has to be a complete chain for an STD to be spread from one person to another. Let me start by explaining the different links. Then, I'll tell you about the puzzle.

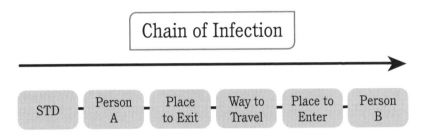

The STD: We've already talked about that piece. STDs are any one of the many diseases that can be transmitted from one person to another through sexual intimacy. Most of them are transmitted through bodily fluids, which includes the fluids a woman's body makes in her vagina, the fluid that a man's body makes (semen) that carries the sperm and that comes out his penis, and blood. There are some exceptions to how some STDs are transmitted, but we'll talk about that in a minute. For now, let's just consider those that are transmitted by sexual fluids. Note, though, that doing anything like sharing dirty needles where your blood gets mixed with blood from an infected person puts you at just as much risk as having sex with an infected person.

Person A: In the chain of infection, one person has to be infected to infect someone else. But for the STD to get to Person B, it has to have a place to leave person A, a way to travel, and a place to enter Person B for Person B to become infected.

Let's talk about the place the STD leaves Person A and the place it enters Person B because these are similar. In general, STDs like warm, moist places. Now think about your bodies for a minute. How many warm, moist openings do you have? Any of these can become exits or entries for an STD if the disease is present. I'll explain more about that in a minute, but first, let's add in the "way to travel." As I mentioned earlier, most STDs travel through either blood or the sexual fluids. So you can get an STD by making contact with an infected person's blood, such as by sharing a dirty needle or sometimes a mom can pass an STD to her baby during delivery. But let's talk more about the sexual fluids.

If Person A and Person B have sex, obviously these fluids go back and forth between the two of them. However, suppose Person A and Person B are just touching each other intimately. Maybe B is just touching A's sexual organs, getting A's fluids on his hands. Maybe then, though, he touches his own body, such as rubbing his eyes, touching his mouth, or touching his own sexual organs. The STD doesn't care how it gets to B's warm, moist openings nor does it care which warm, moist opening it enters. This is very important to understand. You can get an STD from an infected person just by touching or kissing in areas where the infected fluids are. You don't necessarily have to "go all the way" to get infected. This means that intimate touching, oral sex and anal sex can put you at just as much risk for getting an STD as having vaginal intercourse.

Now the puzzle part: Where can you break this chain so that Person A doesn't pass an STD to Person B? (I'll give you one hint: You can't separate a person from his own entry or exit parts.)

Let's explore some of the possibilities and see if we can discover what works. One option would be to break the chain between the "place of exit" and "way to travel." Here's what that would look like:

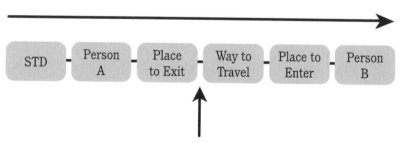

To separate the chain here would mean that Person A finds out she has an STD and does the only responsible thing. She makes a decision not to have sexual contact with anyone else until she is cured, if this is bacterial and curable, or not to have sexual contact again, if this is a virus that cannot be cured. That means that Person A is going to keep anyone else from touching the areas where the infection is. Important reminder: This means halting more than just intercourse. It includes touching and kissing infected areas.

Although this is the most responsible option the infected person has, the problem with this answer is that many infected people don't know they have an STD until major damage has occurred. But even though they don't know they are infected, they can still infect another person. This is certainly not the best answer to the puzzle.

Here is another possible answer:

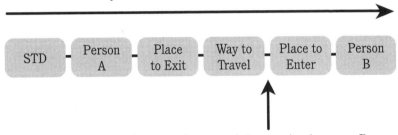

This answer means that sexual contact is happening between Person A and Person B because fluids are leaving A's body. But the fluids don't go into B's body. How could that happen? You've probably heard of this as "practicing safer sex." "Safer sex" means using a condom, which is a latex covering that the man puts over his penis, sort of like putting on a surgical glove. It is very thin and stretchy so that it goes on easily. Its purpose is to block the fluids from going between Person A and Person B.

Two problems with this answer:

Problem 1: When couples use condoms regularly for birth control to prevent pregnancy, condoms fail to prevent pregnancy about one out of six times.[9] That means that one out of six times a condom breaks, tears, leaks, comes off, etc. so that the man's fluids, which carry his sperm, get to the woman, and she becomes pregnant. That's like playing Russian roulette.

Would you do that? Of course not! But that is the same risk you take with condom use alone for preventing pregnancy. The HIV virus, which causes AIDS, is much, much smaller than the sperm that causes pregnancy. Imagine that you are looking at a sperm and HIV virus side by side under a microscope. You have magnified the image until the sperm looks to be the size of a tennis ball. The HIV virus would look about the size of a pencil eraser – tiny in comparison to the sperm. So if the sperm can find its way through or around a condom about one out of six times, what do you think the HIV virus can do?

Problem 2: Although most STDs travel through blood or sexual fluids, there are exceptions. Herpes, which causes the painful sores; syphilis, which destroys your brain and nervous system; and HPV, which causes most cervical cancer cases and kills two times more women each year than AIDS all have a different way of traveling. These three travel by skin-to-skin contact. These three live on the surface of the skin of an infected person. If Person A has one of these and Person B touches or rubs against the infected area, Person B can get the disease. Person A can have Herpes, for instance, in areas that a condom doesn't cover. The condom cannot protect against an area that it does not guard even when it works correctly.

Even health messages that you hear have changed in the past few years. At first when the health professionals started really pushing for everyone to use condoms, they called it "safe sex." Now, though, these messages will say to practice "safer sex" by using a condom. That is a subtle difference, but very important. You see, condom use is not truly safe. It is merely safer than having sex without any protection at all.

There is only one other option to the puzzle.

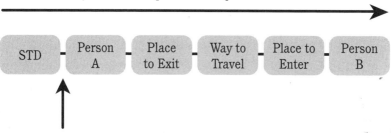

Breaking the chain here would mean that Person A and Person B are having sex, but they do not have an STD to worry about. Can that happen? Can a man and woman enjoy having sex together without ever having to worry about an STD between them? Sure! But how? Ah, another puzzle for you.

"Well," you might answer, "if both are sure they don't have an STD before they have sex together, then they don't have to worry, right?"

Right! But how can they be sure? Hopefully, by now you know that you can't always tell whether someone is infected by looking at him or by assessing how he feels because most infected people do not have any symptoms until long after they have been infected. What if Person B just asks Person A if she has ever been with anyone else before? Would you trust your health and your life to someone's answer? What if that person was drinking and doesn't remember what he did? Just taking someone's word for it is risky business these days.

What if that person has only been with, say, one or two people. That's not much risk, right? Let's think about that one a minute. It is true that the fewer people you have been with sexually, the lower your risk. However, imagine that you are thinking about having sex with this person who says he has been with only two other people. Now suppose that each of those two people has been with only two other people. And we continue that pattern just three more times.

Think About It

How's your math? How many people, counting the person you are thinking about and all the other people involved, would be in this chain if that happened?

The answer? 63. And how many of those 63 people would have to be infected to put you at risk if you say yes to this person? It takes only one to put the whole bunch at risk. You see, you aren't just risking what might have been a problem for one or two people; you are exposing yourself to everyone who is connected by this chain.

What about just getting tested first? Again, this is not a perfect answer because some STDs can take up to six months or more to show up on a test, but the person can still be contagious. That would mean the person would have had to have no sexual contact (including intimate touching or kissing) with anyone for at least six months and then be tested to be fairly sure that everything is okay. That can work, but it takes a lot of time.

Think About It

• What if neither Person A nor Person B has ever been with anyone else sexually (including touching and kissing in genital areas), and they come together and have sex and never have sex with anyone else except each other for life – do they have to worry about an STD? (This assumes, again, that blood contact has not occurred either.)

- Can these two people enjoy sex with each other without ever having to worry "till death do they part"?

- What do we call this kind of relationship?

This is marriage! The only way to enjoy God's perfect and wonderful gift of sex without the worries of all of these diseases is by closing the bond of marriage around you and your spouse before either of you ever begins exploring, touching and kissing intimately with anyone.

God knew exactly what it would take to see that "none of these diseases" plagued our lives and our marriages. This same loving God who protected the Israelites from the diseases of Egypt has given us what we need to protect our lives from these horrible, life-threatening diseases. He knew and told us what to do long before the doctors figured it out. Our Creator, our Father, knows just what we need.

Summing It Up

Can you see the hand of our love-light-spirit God in this? He knows how we are formed and what risks we face if we step outside of His design for us. The limitations He places on us are out of love and concern for our well-being. He loves us enough to warn us and to guide us so that we can avoid some of the pain that Satan is trying his best to inflict on us.

Talk About It

1. What in this study was different from what you have heard in the world? What surprised you?

2. Has the discussion about how STDs are transmitted changed what you would consider as "safe sex?"

3. How does it feel to know that God is concerned about protecting you from these harmful effects of sex outside of marriage?

Pray About It

Thank You, our amazing Lord, for the protection You offer us through Your Word. Help us to trust You more and more as we see Your love displayed for us in Your guidance. Give us wisdom, Lord, to see past Satan's lies that try to tempt us into a deadly, casual approach to sex, which seeks to destroy its wonderful blessing in marriage.

Chapter 10

Am I Ready?

Opening Reflections

A little more than two years into marriage, I was eager to welcome our firstborn into our family. Nine long months of pregnancy preceded by the anguish of a miscarriage had me longing to hold this baby in my arms. In no way was I prepared for what was to follow. My sweet little newborn spent more hours yelling at the top of his tiny lungs than I thought was humanly possible. I would nurse him, after which he would promptly spit up pretty much everything he had taken in. I'd clean up him, me and the ceiling and then lay him down for a short nap before he woke up howling again. Repeat the cycle. This was our life for about six weeks. There is absolutely no way I could have gotten through this physically and emotionally exhausting time without my incredibly loving, patient husband at my side.

Starting Point

Think for a minute about all of the roles and responsibilities you have in your life. For example, if you are a teen or young adult, then you are a member of a family. Perhaps you are also a student and/or a member of a club or a sports team. Perhaps you have a special hobby or talent you like to spend time doing. If you are an adult, you may have some of these same responsibilities, but you may also have a job and/or have to care for your home or for elderly family members.

Think About It

Take a minute and list as many of these types of activities and responsibilities as you can think of that you spend time doing on a regular basis (at least one time per week.)

Now, grab a paper plate (or draw a circle about that size). Imagine that this circle represents your week. How much time do you spend each week on each of the things you have listed? Divide the circle into different size "pie pieces" to represent how each of those roles fit into your week. Don't forget to include sleeping, eating, etc. in your week's pie. You use some of your week doing those things too.

Think About It

• What piece of pie is largest for you?

• Are there pieces that you wish were larger or smaller?

• How hard was it to draw this pie? What were the challenges?

Now, imagine that you suddenly have the responsibility of a newborn. The baby is yours. Take a second paper plate or piece of paper with a new circle and decide how you will make this new responsibility fit into your week's pie. Hint: Newborn babies take a LOT of time! And it's not fair to just pass the baby off to Grandma or Grandpa or another baby sitter unless you have a job that can pay for childcare. Also, even if you have a way of paying for childcare, keep in mind that the baby will be home with you at night or on weekends or whenever you are off duty from your job.

Think About It

• How big a slice of pie did you put for the new baby?

• What had to change to make that piece fit?

• What would be the hardest part of having a baby for you right now?

A few years ago, a couple did a study where they asked real families to do the activity you just did.[1] They asked husbands and wives to complete the chart before their first baby was born and then after their first baby was 18 months old. Below are four pies. One for men before the baby was born and one for after the baby was 18 months, and then one for women at each of the same two points.

Can you guess which chart goes with which role (husband or wife) at which time (before or after the baby)? For the sake of simplicity, the roles that are shown are "Partner," which means time for each other as husband and wife; "Worker," which means the time they spent in a paid job; "Parent," which means time devoted to taking care of the baby or to getting ready for the baby before it was born; and "Other," which is just all the other kinds of things they did (hobbies, clubs, extra activities) lumped together.

You can check your answers on the next page.

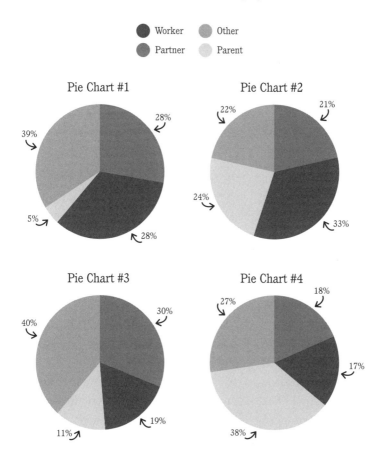

Answer Key:
- Pie No. 1: Husbands before the baby was born.
- Pie No. 2: Husbands when the baby was 18 months old.
- Pie No. 3: Wives before the baby was born.
- Pie No. 4: Wives when the baby was 18 months old.

 Think About It

- Why do you think husbands and wives responded differently?

- Do you see any of God's planned roles for families reflected in these charts?

- What surprised you most about these responses?

- How do you think it would be different for a woman if she didn't have a husband when her baby was born?

- How do you think it would be different for a man if he wasn't married to the woman who had his baby? What if he was the primary caregiver? What if the mom was, but they did not live together?

- What would be different if either the mom or dad were still in high school or college?

In case you don't know it by now, let me tell you a secret: Caring for a baby is a huge challenge! It is amazing how one little bitty baby can change your life so much. Your roles shift, how you spend your money changes, the amount of sleep you get diminishes, the amount of stuff you have to take with you to go on even a short trip to the store multiplies. Pretty much everything you do shifts to make room for this new little life. In fact, pregnancy rounds out the top 12 stressors for adults on the Holmes and Rahe Stress Scale (a widely used stress rating) and is tied for first place for teens.

Given that adding a new baby to a family is a significant challenge for adults, how do teenagers do when they face this same responsibility? Let's explore that answer across five areas.

First, let's talk about the health of the baby and mom. During the teen years, a girl's body is growing and changing rapidly, requiring a huge demand on her body just to keep up with her own growth. Adding the increased demand of a baby's growth inside this young woman greatly increases the potential for lots of health troubles. This double demand often means that either the mom or the baby's body loses out.

As a result, teen moms are more likely to have a miscarriage or premature birth than adult women. Babies born prematurely often experience birth defects or long hospital stays to help their tiny bodies get ready to make it on their own. And even those babies who make it through the birth process have an increased risk of death in the first year. [2]

Let's look now at education and money, which are closely tied together. First, 60 to 70 percent of teen moms and dads end up dropping out of school. This greatly reduces their chances of getting a good paying job. As a result, more than three-fourths of teen moms end up on public assistance (welfare, TANF, food stamps, SNAP) before the baby is 5 years old. Most of them just can't make ends meet on their own.

Although each state varies on what a mom can get from public assistance, I assure you it isn't much. Chances are, if that's all the resources a mom and her baby have, they will still be very poor. Even with a high school education, a single mom is significantly more likely to live in poverty with her children. In fact, poverty rates are highest for households headed by a single woman than any other family type, twice as high as households headed by single men and five times higher than married couple households. [3]

Think About It

- Would you feel prepared to care for a baby who was born with significant health problems? What would be the hardest part of that?

- Make a list of everything you can think of that you would need to care for a baby for a month. Take your list to the store, and see what all of that would cost. Or ask someone who has had a baby recently what those things cost. How would you pay those expenses?

Read About It

1 Timothy 5:8

Think About It

- What does God expect us to do for our family?

- How does this apply to someone when he or she is making a choice about having sex or not?

Here, God makes it clear that He expects us to take care of our families. So choosing to have sex means being ready and able to accept the responsibility of caring for a child if a pregnancy occurs.

Then, there is the legal issue. Each state has a law in place that addresses what is called "statutory rape." What that means is that the government is working to protect young people from the dangers of sex at an early age. "Statutory rape" is a term used to describe sexual relations involving a person who is considered too young to give legal consent. You probably know there are some things you can't legally do before age 18, such as get a loan for a car, join the army, etc. That is because, by law, young people are protected against making those decisions at too young an age. The same is true for sex. Although state laws differ, you will find that each state has some kind of penalty for having sex with someone who is considered too young.

Sometimes that means someone older than 18 having sex with someone younger than 18. But in some states, age difference is a factor too. For instance, there may be a 24-month statement that says if anyone has sex with someone under age 18 and there is more than 24 months difference, the older person can be charged. If that is the case in your state, suppose a 15-year-old girl is dating a 17-year-old boy, and they have sex. The boy could be charged and possibly go to jail.

You may be thinking, "Yeah, but she's not going to turn her boyfriend in." True, perhaps, but what if she gets pregnant? Or what if her daddy finds out? Or what if she breaks up with him and is mad at him? And keep in mind that if the girl is older, she can be the one charged too. This can mean real trouble for a really long time. What if the younger person wanted to have sex? What if he pushed in that direction? The law says that doesn't matter. Too young is too young regardless of whose idea it was.

 ## Read About It
Romans 13:1-4

 ## Think About It
• What has God said about obeying the laws of the land?

• How does His guidance fit with this discussion?

An Example

Janet spent much of her teenage years bouncing from boyfriend to boyfriend, never content unless she had some guy at her side. She would do anything to keep a guy's attention. By the time she was 18, she was pregnant with her first child. Her daughter's dad stayed around for only a short time before he left Janet to care for their child alone. Janet found herself having to move back into her parents' house to make ends meet. She began to work and to try to finish school, but in her early 20s, she became involved with another man. During the next two years, he walked in and out of her life. Two children later, he finally walked away for good, taking one of their children with him.

Now in legal battles, she struggles with the heartache of not seeing her second born child. Meanwhile, she is still dependent on her own parents for financial, emotional and physical support in raising her two children who are with her. At a time when her peers are completing college degrees, beginning careers, and launching into marriage, Janet is spending time in lawyers' offices battling her ex-boyfriend and seeking public assistance to meet her financial needs. Although she loves her children dearly, she knows that her early choices have put her on this rough road.

Janet's story is just one example of how making choices against God's plan leads to pain that is heartbreaking. God knows that, and He is seeking to save us from this pain. But it is not just about the pain of this life. Our choices also lead to spiritual consequences. How does God feel about all of this? He has given us clear guidance.

Read About It

1 Corinthians 6:18-20

Think About It

• What did God say about sexual immorality or fornication (having sex with someone who is not your spouse)?

• Why is fornication a sin against your own body?

• In verse 19, God stated that our bodies are temples of the Holy Spirit and that we are not our own. What does having sex outside of marriage do to that relationship?

As you prayerfully consider all that we have studied in this lesson, you can see once again that when God put sex within a marriage, He was choosing to act out of love for us, knowing that having a child as a single parent or as a young parent is extremely difficult and even dangerous. Our Father knew that we would need the support of a loving spouse to help us raise our children.

One final note: "I'll just use birth control" isn't going to solve this one. Even when used perfectly, birth control is not a 100-percent guarantee that you won't get pregnant. All forms of birth control can and do fail at times. The only guarantee is to not have sex.

Ending a life with abortion is certainly no good answer either. No one walks away from that choice without scars. Knowing you have taken a life that was once in you is an unbelievable burden to carry for the rest of your life.

Summing It Up

I pray that as we have walked through the potential consequences of sex outside of marriage, you can see the consistent evidence of God's love for you as He clearly guides us onto a path of sexual purity. God knows better than any human the pains that await us when we take Satan's bait and go off in the wrong direction. God wants to protect us from that pain. Yet He still allows us the freedom to choose. So choose wisely, considering His love for you as His daughter.

 Talk About It

1. If you have ever baby-sat for someone's children, how long did you stay before you were tired and ready to go home? What was the hardest part?

2. What are some benefits that a baby with a married mom and dad has compared to a baby of a young, single mom?

 Pray About It

Dear Father, we are so grateful to be Your children. We thank You for designing the family in such a way that Your littlest children are best protected and nurtured. We ask Your blessings on all our families and on all our hearts as we learn to trust Your love and wisdom more and more.

Chapter 11

Living the Message

Opening Reflections

Bryan and Bethany made a decision that was noticeably different from their peers. Yet their decision had an incredible impact on everyone around them. I'll come back to their story later.

Starting Point

Have you ever watched a home video or a silly movie where you knew what was going to happen before it happened? What thoughts were going through your mind as you watched?

We've been working through two big ideas so far. The first one is that because God loves us, He designed us with a plan in mind that was for our benefit, not just to restrict our fun. The second big idea is that when we step outside of God's loving plan, some very real dangers arise. God knew this. Just as you can sit back and predict what will happen on a home video or silly movie, God – Master of the universe – can sit above all things and see where our choices will lead. That is why He has given us guidelines for navigating around the dangers this life holds.

Accepting these truths, we will move now to living the message God has provided. It is one thing to understand guidelines; it is something else to actually live them. This is especially true in living sexually pure lives. Our world in no way supports this lifestyle. So how are we supposed to put God's plan to work in our lives? Good news: He helps us with that part too.

In our sex-saturated world, we get bombarded by either in-your-face messages or at least hints of sex on a daily basis. Let's talk about these for a minute because they will help us consider some important boundaries. Grab a piece of paper, and answer a couple of questions to help us get started. Chances are you have already begun to recognize some of the hints that guys offer girls when they have sex on their minds.

Question 1: What are some things a guy does to give a girl a hint he has sex on his mind? Make a list of these, and be as specific as you can.

A few years ago, I was teaching a series of lessons similar to these at a Christian summer camp to a group of teen girls. At the same time, my husband was teaching the teen guys. We asked the girls to answer the same question you just answered, but the guys answered this question: "What are some things a girl does to give a guy a hint she has sex on her mind?"

Question 2: How do you think the guys answered this question? Be specific.

Now, look at your two lists side by side. Do you see any differences? Let's see how your answers stack up against what the guys actually said. Go to the chart on the next page and read their answers.

Think About It

- Did any of their responses surprise you? If so, which ones? What was surprising about them?

- Were there any differences between your list and the guys' list? If so, what were some of the main differences you noticed? Why do you think those are there? How do they relate to what we have studied so far about the differences between guys and girls?

- One of the guys responded by saying, "It's not necessarily what we can see, but what we can almost see." How should this insight change the way girls choose to dress?

Guys' List

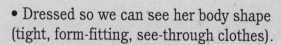

- Dressed so we can see her body shape (tight, form-fitting, see-through clothes).
- Showing her cleavage, tummy or crack.
- Showing off her breasts.
- Being flirty, acting sexy.
- Encouraging us to touch her.
- Acting vulnerable or helpless.
- Walking to get attention.
- Wearing short skirts, skirts with a split, or shorts.

Read About It

Ephesians 5:3-5

In this case, the New International Version (1984) makes verse 3 jump off the page. Here is what it says: "But among you there must not be *even a hint of sexual immorality*, or of any kind of impurity, or of greed, because these are improper for God's holy people" (emphasis added). That's pretty clear, isn't it? Not even a hint. What gives a hint that someone is thinking about sex? Look back over your list, and think about this for a minute.

I want to share one response from an honest heart. At the close of this lesson during the camp session, one young woman asked to be excused to go back to the cabin. When I asked her why she needed to go back, she explained that she needed to change her shirt. She had read the boys' list and knew she was violating the "not even a hint" guideline by the way she was dressed. She wanted to correct that message as soon as she could.

So what about your closet? If you were to take the guys' list and measure each of your clothing items against what they see as hints, would you make changes? Unfortunately, we women cannot measure ourselves by ourselves (what other women think or wear). Women are very poor judges of what gives a hint to a guy, just as guys are poor judges of what gives a hint to a girl. So if you are sincere about living a life with not even a hint of sexual immorality, forget what you see other women wear or what is fashionable. Instead, focus your attention on what gives guys hints. Notice that their list is almost all about what they see, in keeping with a guy's tendency to be attracted to visual stimulation. This is sometimes hard for a girl to see. However, if your dad, brother or another godly male indicates your outfit is questionable or inappropriate, listen, and go change your clothes.

Think About It

- What is the reason God stated we should not even give a hint of sexual immorality?

- How does "not even a hint" look different from the world's standards for dress? for immorality?

- Notice that Ephesians 5:4 also cautions against obscenity, foolish talk, and even coarse joking. How would following this guidance change your conversations with friends, music choices, and TV and movie viewing?

The idea that these hints are "improper for God's holy people" (v. 4 NIV84) is a very significant idea we need to consider. Does the idea of being holy scare you? Does it seem unreachable? The word "holy" means "set apart" or "different." It doesn't take a lot of imagination to see that living a life that does not include even a hint of these activities would set a person apart from the way the world lives. In that way, we become holy. It's not being different just for the sake of being different; it's being different in trust and obedience to God's loving guidance. Our faith in His plan leads us to act, dress and talk differently from the world.

God added another thought in this passage that we need to consider. Look at Ephesians 5:5 again: "No immoral, impure or greedy person – such a man is an idolater – has any inheritance in the kingdom of Christ and of God" (NIV84). Do you know what an idolater is? That is someone who worships something or someone other than God. In this verse God said living an immoral or impure life is the same as being an idolater and living as an idolater keeps us from having a place in God's kingdom. That's pretty serious stuff, don't you think?

Think About It

- How is following after sexual impurity the same as idolatry? What would the person be worshiping?

- Why do you think idolatry is so terrible to God that it removes a person from His kingdom?

Insights From Bethany

Justifying hints of sexual immorality but still saying you won't go "all the way" is like finding a recipe and preheating the oven without actually baking anything. Why set the stage? Imagine that your life is being documented in a random snapshot format. If certain actions or thoughts became a snapshot on display for others to see with no background or follow-up, would spectators assume that you were living a sexually immoral lifestyle? "Not even a hint" suggests living above reproach. Don't think about how you would have a perfectly valid argument should you be questioned. Save time and your reputation by not putting yourself in a situation that would bring about suspicion of sin in the first place.

Read About It
Ephesians 5:1-2

Think About It

- What did God call us in Ephesians 5:1-2?

- How does reading verses 1-2 put the restrictions in verses 3-5 into context?

Yes, God has standards for us, but we are continually reminded that these are because we are "dearly loved children" (Ephesians 5:1 NIV84). No loving parent in the world allows his children to do anything they want without offering guidance to protect and nurture them. Anything else would simply not be love. God knows that living a life of (or even hinting of) sexual immorality, impurity or greed is going to lead us down a path of emotional hurt, disappointment, possibly physical pain or death, and ultimately spiritual death. He does not want that for us. So as a loving Father, He guides us to stay far away from it all.

To illustrate, the other day I was channel surfing and came across an old black and white movie. Although I didn't watch enough to know even what the movie was, a short scene grabbed my attention. Here's what happened: A man was visiting a friend on a large farm. The visitor decided to take a walk outside for a few minutes. As he strolled along a path in a wooded section, another rather scruffy-looking man jumped out in front of him and ordered him to stop in his tracks. The visitor immediately took a defensive posture and held his walking cane up in defense.

The scruffy guy grabbed the cane and slammed the tip into the ground just inches in front of the visitor, springing a deadly steel trap. The scruffy guy's voice softened as he warned the visitor that many people set traps in the area and that the visitor needed to be very cautious. He went on to warn the visitor that there was an area ahead, just off the trail, that had patches of slimy mud that would quickly engulf anyone who stepped into it. "Stay on the trail, and you will be okay."

Well, of course, the visitor got off the trail and, within seconds, was sinking, fighting for his life in one of the mud pits. The scruffy guy ran to the visitor's aid as soon as he heard his cry and began to work frantically to free him from the trap. Why did the visitor get off the trail? He saw a pretty woman and went chasing after her.

Think About It

- What motivated the scruffy guy to halt the visitor? Was he being cruel, bullying, restrictive or selfish in what he said?

- How about the visitor? How do you think his opinion of the scruffy guy changed over the course of this encounter?

- How does this little story illustrate our relationship with God?

- What kinds of people, situations or conversations cause you to ignore previous warnings and wander off the path? Brainstorm ways to avoid those distractions.

God is there for us, working to protect and care for us as His children. He seeks to show us the traps. He warns us of the dangers ahead.

And He runs to our aid when we call. Does that mean He removes the traps Satan has set? No. Does that mean He stops us from making our own choices? No. It does mean He provides us with what we need to steer clear of these, but He leaves in our hands the freedom of choice.

Read About It
Ephesians 5:15-16

Think About It
• What does it mean to be wise?

• How does following God's direction demonstrate wisdom?

As I watched the movie, I just shook my head when the visitor left the path and took off running after the woman. I knew what was coming. Of course, it was no surprise to me when he fell into the mud pit. I started a conversation in my head with the visitor: "Well, what did you expect? You were warned by someone who knew what was out there. He had already proved that he was trying to protect you. Why didn't you listen?"

But aren't we often just like the visitor? God knows this world – He created it. And He knows Satan's traps. Here's what He said to us: "Be careful how you walk" (Ephesians 5:15). "Let no one deceive you with empty words" (v. 6). "Do not be foolish, but understand what the will of the Lord is" (v. 17) because you are "beloved children" (v. 1).

The Rest of the Story
Bryan and Bethany's relationship was always a little bit different. On their very first date, they sat on a dock overlooking a dazzling blue lake while committing to some dating "ground rules." It was important to both of them, from the very beginning, to commit to a relationship that was pleasing to God and obedient to His standards. Early on, that meant reading from His Word together, praying for His guidance, and individually establishing accountable relationships to keep them on a path of integrity and righteousness.

It also meant abstaining from the commonly accepted intimacy of kissing, which even some of their closest friends didn't understand.

"Yes," they would say, "I agree that you shouldn't make out, but … you aren't going to kiss at all?"

Nope, not at all. Because their continual goal was to be completely pure before the Lord and each other, they learned that being
"extreme" was totally worth the greatly anticipated moment when
the minister finally said "You may now kiss your bride" on their
wedding day. As a witness to that special moment, I can tell you
that the joy was tangible as many of us knew what that kiss meant.

"Not even a hint" of sexual immorality will mean breaking away from
the mold of what everyone else is doing. As you may have guessed,
this is the same Bethany who provides insights throughout this book.
Here is what she said:

Insights From Bethany

Although the world views "going all the way" as giving in to lust and
temptation completely and unreservedly, I am working on "going all the
way" for Christ. In other words, I am not apologizing for taking drastic
measures to avoid sexual sin but rather choosing to truly "flee youthful
lusts" as the scripture urges (2 Timothy 2:22). Notice that it doesn't say
to merely "tip toe around" or even "stay and fight against" youthful
lusts. Instead, do what it takes (go all the way) to NOT open the door
to compromise no matter how unpopular, seemingly "overboard," or
uncomfortable it may be to others around you (or even, at times, to you).

Summing It Up

God, our loving Father, knows the dangers we face. In His love, He
guides us to imitate Him – walk in His steps – so we can avoid the traps
and pain that would engulf us. Please note: He is not suggesting that we
stay only inches away from the traps. He says to stay way far away – not
even a hint of being near the traps. He loves us too much not to warn us
of the pain that is out there when we choose to step outside of His guidance. When we choose His path, we are also influencing those around us
to walk in the safety of His guidance. As such, we are also living a life of
love as imitators of God (Ephesians 5:1). I like knowing where the mud
pits and traps are, don't you?

Talk About It

1. Has this study of Ephesians 5 changed or confirmed your understanding of the purity God expects of you? In what ways?

2. What do you think people around you might do or say to discourage you from taking God's path of purity? How can you respond to those challenges?

3. What will you do differently, if anything, because of this lesson?

Pray About It

Thank You, dear, sweet Father, for protecting us from the harmful traps that Satan has set for us. Thank You, too, Lord, for being ready to run to our sides when we call out to You, even when we have been foolish and stepped outside of Your guidance. We thank You for forgiving us and lifting us from the mud pits of our mistakes to set us back on Your path in love. Help us to remember constantly that Your guidance is evidence of Your love for us.

Recommended Reading

• ***Boy Meets Girl*** by Joshua Harris (Colorado Springs: Multnomah Books, 2005). *Boy Meets Girl* deals with all the tough questions that come once a couple thinks they are ready to pursue a relationship with the ultimate goal of marriage in mind from the very beginning. Harris wrote the book one year after marrying his wife and tells how the principles of biblical courtship worked in their lives.

• ***I Kissed Dating Goodbye*** by Joshua Harris (Colorado Springs: Multnomah Books, 1997). One of the great quotes from the book is "I view dating in a similar light as I view fast-food restaurants – it's not wrong to eat there, but something far better is available." Practical discussions and challenges help explore the importance of pursuing a mature relationship with God without letting the obstacles accompanying traditional dating to get in the way.

Chapter 12

Frogs and Roller Coasters

Opening Reflections

I heard a story once that made a deep impression on my memory. The story took place in a remote village perched high on a mountaintop. The school that served the village sat near the bottom of the mountain with only one treacherous narrow road connecting the two. As the beginning of the school year approached, an announcement went out about a job opening for a bus driver who would be charged with making the daily trip up and down the mountain.

Only three applicants were willing to consider the dangerous task. As a part of the interview process, the school administrator put all three applicants on the bus and asked them to take turns driving the big vehicle up and down the narrow trek. The first applicant chose to demonstrate his ability to make the trip in record time. He lurched the bus forward, rounding curves and shooting rapidly up the straights. Sure enough, he broke all records for making the trip. He could certainly get the children to school in record time.

The second applicant, not to be outdone by the first, chose to demonstrate his agility in handling the massive bus. He nimbly maneuvered the bus inches from guardrails and a hand's breadth from steep drop-offs. He got closer to the edges than anyone else could, yet without a single scratch or dent to the bus. Clearly, he had the best skill in maneuvering close to the edges.

Taking his turn, the final applicant quietly took his place behind the wheel. He drove slowly and steadily around the curves and narrow passes. When he neared a guardrail or bridge, he stayed as far from the edge as possible. The trip was completely uneventful to the point that the administrator and other two applicants found themselves dozing a bit toward the end. Puzzled by the mild display of skill, the administrator asked the applicant why he had taken this approach.

"Simple," the man replied, "I wanted to show how far from danger's edge I could stay."

He got the job.

I wonder how often we see just how close to the edge we can get? Think about that as we consider frogs and roller coasters.

Starting Point

Imagine for a moment that a young man truly loves a woman in his life. He has demonstrated pure love to her by caring for her, doing thoughtful things for her, helping her when she was facing challenges, and reaching out to her as a friend. If the woman accepts that love, how will she respond? What if she rejects his love? How will that look?

We've spent a lot of time up to this point thinking about God's love for us and how He always chooses what is best for us in keeping with His perfect love. But how do we respond back to Him? Do we accept that love or reject it? In this lesson, we will examine some of the ways we can demonstrate to God that we accept His gift of love for us.

 ## Read About It
1 Thessalonians 4:1-2

 ## Think About It
• What is the point of what God is getting ready to say here (v. 1)?

• What do the words "more and more" (NKJV or ESV) or "excel still more" (NASB) in verse 1 mean to you?

Just like the young man in our Starting Point, God has offered us pure love. So now, we are at a point of decision in considering our response. Have you ever been interested in a guy and tried to figure out how to demonstrate your interest in him? Been there. I remember one guy in college whom I really wanted to notice me, but I never could figure out how to get his attention. How frustrating to try to guess how to demonstrate love to another person. But God didn't leave us to guess about how to demonstrate acceptance of His love. In these few short verses that we will explore, God gave us a picture of how we can respond to His love in very clear terms.

Read About It
1 Thessalonians 4:3-5

God started by giving us a context, a realm in which we will be talking. Verse 3 is pretty plain in saying that we are to avoid sexual immorality. God, in His love, wants this hedge around our lives because He knows the pain that is on the other side. But He didn't just stop by saying, "Don't do it." He actually talked about some areas to help guide our steps.

The first realm that concerns God is our own bodies (vessels). God wants us to know how to control our own bodies, not just "go with the flow" in what we choose to do. And He put this control in our brains. Notice that He said we should "learn" or "know" (depending on which version you may be reading) how to control our bodies.

Think About It
- Why do you think God put the challenge of controlling our bodies in our brain?

- How does this differ from the advice to "follow your heart" or "do what feels good"?

- Why is getting your brain involved in channeling your life toward purity so important?

The words "sanctified" or "holy" mean living a life that is set apart from the world around us. We will look different. Our emotions can be, let's face it, really crummy guides for making wise choices sometimes. I'm sure you can easily think of at least one girl who flits about from guy to guy "following her heart" but clearly not engaging her brain in the process.

Love is about choice, brain power – not fluttering emotions. Understand that I am not suggesting we all should become emotionless robots. However, we have to get our heads in the game if we are going to become truly holy. Choosing holiness – choosing to be set apart from the world – will lead us to lives that are honorable. Now, does that mean that everyone will automatically praise and respect us when we choose to live pure lives? I hope you know the answer to that question is no. Satan, and those whom he can influence, will always try to tear down anything that is good. When you stand up to a life of purity, there will be those who try to talk you down to their level.

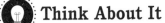 **Think About It**

• What are some of the things people might say to you to get you to step away from your stand for purity?

• How can you prepare for those challenges?

Hold those thoughts for a few moments while we take a look at the second realm God described in these few verses.

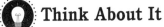 **Read About It**

1 Thessalonians 4:6

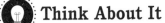 **Think About It**

• How can someone mistreat or take advantage of someone else in the area of sexual purity?

• How serious is it if I lead someone else in the wrong direction in this area?

• Why do you think God holds us accountable for how we influence someone else?

God loves all of us. He loves His daughters and His sons. He is pleased when we respond to Him by learning to control our own bodies sexually, and He is equally pleased when we expand our love to Him by protecting those around us. However, His disappointment in us when we lead someone else into sin is clear. By leading someone else into sin, we are leading them away from God's love. How much pain that causes our Father! That's not what He had in mind. He calls us to something greater, more beautiful.

Read About It
1 Thessalonians 4:7-8

Think About It
- What do you think it means for God to "call" us to a holy life or holiness? Why does He call us to holiness?

- How does He see our rejection of His guidance?

- Have you ever been rejected after truly trying to show someone kindness and love? How did you feel?

Think of it like this: Imagine you are going to throw a huge party and you want all of your friends and loved ones to come celebrate with you. So you invite them all to join you. If people want to be with you, they will be excited to have the invitation and feel honored to have been invited. But how will they respond if they really don't like you much or want to be with you? This mirrors God's call or invitation to us. He loves us and is calling us to be where He is – in holiness – so we can be with Him and celebrate with Him. If we want to be with Him, then we will choose to accept the call to be where He is. You see, God is pure. He cannot join us in a sinful life. But He can call us to join Him where He is – a choice He makes in love.

These few verses help us see how important it is to give some really honest thought to how we will manage our own bodies in sexual purity and how we will interact with others so as not to tempt them away from purity. So what does sexual purity look like? How do we learn to control our bodies and not tempt others? Before we go deeply into those questions, let's look at what often happens in dating relationships.

Riding the Roller Coaster

Think About It
Have you ever done something that really gave you butterflies in your stomach?

Maybe it was speaking up in class or getting on a roller coaster for the first time or flying in an airplane. Although we are all created differently with different fears and comfort levels, the truth is we all have tried things that caused us to have a bit of butterflies, right?

Those "butterflies," as we call them, are the result of adrenaline, which is a chemical released into our blood when we are facing something that is new, scary or exciting. It is there for our protection in that it can help us get through a particularly difficult or new situation. This same adrenaline is released when you slip and almost fall off a steep hill, when a car weaves over toward you unexpectedly, and when your little brother or sister jumps out from the closet and startles you. Adrenaline gives you an extra boost of energy and even physical strength to respond to a threat or challenge. So it is good within its designed purpose.

Think About It

What happens to those feelings when you keep doing the thing that caused them?

Here's where adrenaline can cause confusion in dating relationships. First, let's go back to the roller coaster or airplane trip or whatever it was. Let's say you ride that roller coaster for the first time. What a rush! When you get off, you run back around and get in line again. When it's your turn to get on – there's that rush again. But what happens if you keep getting back on – maybe several times that day or maybe even several times spread out over a bunch of days? Do you have the same feeling of excitement that you did the first time you rode? Probably not.

At some point, if we keep doing what causes the "rush," we eventually become accustomed to whatever it is, and it loses some of the excitement that caused adrenaline to be released. So if we still want to experience the "rush," we have to get on a bigger roller coaster or hold our hands up the whole way or something new to get that same excitement back.

What does this have to do with dating and purity? Simple. For most of us, when we first catch that special guy looking our way and smiling, we get the butterflies, right? "He noticed me! I think he might come over and talk to me!" Maybe your face even blushes a little and your palms get sweaty. That's adrenaline. Your body is saying: "Something new and exciting is about to happen. Get ready."

Let's say this guy does walk over and start talking to you. You are nervous at first, but as you continue talking, you really hit it off and find yourself relaxing a bit. As your visit ends, he asks you out. You continue talking over the next few days and begin really relaxing into a friendship. But then, right in the middle of one of your long conversations, he reaches over and holds your hand. There's that adrenaline again. And then, maybe a few dates later, he gives you a kiss on the cheek. Adrenaline surge! But, you see, after a few days of holding hands and good-night kisses, although you will still enjoy them, you will no longer experience the adrenaline release.

So for some couples, they think that signals time to become more intimate in touching and kissing, each change bringing a new adrenaline surge and a new level of excitement. Somewhere in the middle of all of this, couples can quickly begin to mistake the adrenaline rush for feelings of love. Then, if the adrenaline isn't there, they move forward into a more physical relationship to get that same feeling. It is much like the high attributed to drugs. Adrenaline leaves a person feeling excited and upbeat. That's love, right? No. That's adrenaline – a high that comes from a chemical release, not a true sense of wanting what is best for the other person (real love).

This is just one of the reasons why depending on emotions as a relationship guide can get you into a lot of trouble. Remember how God placed the control of your body in your head? He designed you. He knew that this could be confusing.

Deceiving the Frog

So what does that have to do with frogs? (Remember the title of the chapter?) As you might remember from biology class, frogs are cold-blooded creatures, which means they cannot maintain their body temperature on their own. Where the human body can pretty much maintain a 98.6 degree temperature regardless of the external temperature, frogs can't do that. If it is cold around them, their body temperature drops. If it is hot, their body temperature rises. That said, imagine that we have a small frog sitting in front of us. If I were to pick him up and drop him into a pan of boiling water (please don't try this at home), what do you think he would do? He would frantically try to get out, jumping and swimming for all he's worth until he couldn't swim any more (or until I rescued him).

But not wishing to freak out the little frog, what if we set him in a pan of just nicely warm water – not hot or cold, just pleasantly warm? What would he likely do? I'm thinking he would just swim around and enjoy the water. Now, here's the interesting part. I am told – although I haven't tried it (and please don't try this at home) – that if you gently raise the temperature just a bit in the frog's pan, he will still be okay with it even though it is a little warm. His body will adjust to the change, and he will just keep on swimming around contentedly.

But what if we ease the temperature up a bit more – getting a little on the hot side, but not too much? He will continue to swim. It's warm, but his body gets used to the change quickly. So he doesn't make any effort to get out. If you continue very gradually to raise the temperature, I'm told that the frog will never sense the danger but will actually stay content in the water until it becomes hot enough to kill him. You see, because the change was gradual, he never saw the danger coming. His body got used to the danger one degree at a time.

We are frogs. We can easily become deceived into believing that a long chain of little shifts in what we are allowing in our physical relationships with guys isn't really going to hurt anything.

Think About It
Have you ever seen an example of this type of progression?

So many couples get caught up in this progression. They mistake feelings of adrenaline for love and think that they have to have one to have the other. So they keep pushing for something new to keep that excited feeling going. Any time you allow your emotions to overpower your brain, you will not be acting out of *agape* love. Love is a choice, and to act on a choice means to think. When feeling good becomes more important than thinking right, you have left the realm of *agape* love to which God called you. Holiness cannot exist outside of this kind of love because it is the only way we can truly honor God and choose what is right.

Let's get really concrete here in what we are discussing. While I can't describe a chain of events that would be true for every couple that slides down this slope, there is, in general, a progression that is fairly typical.

Think About It
In the chart on the next page is a list of 12 types of physical interaction that might lead a couple down the pathway to sexual impurity. Put them in the order that you think would be the most logical progression. There is really no right or wrong answer to this, but take a minute to think this through. It will help in the next part of this discussion.

_____ Hands to the waist (waist hug)

_____ Hands to the breasts

_____ Hands below the waist

_____ Holding hands

_____ Kiss on the cheek

_____ Kisses to other parts of the body

_____ Long kissing

_____ Looking into each other's eyes

_____ Moving or removing clothes

_____ Sexual intercourse

_____ Short kiss on the lips

_____ Shoulder hug

Now, as you think about this progression, look at the questions below, and think about where you would draw the line for each.

- Where do you think a dating couple your age should stop?
- Where do you think an engaged couple should stop?
- At what point are you putting your physical body at risk?
- At what point are you putting your heart (emotions) at risk?
- At what point is a guy likely to be tempted?
- At what point is a girl likely to be tempted?
- Where do you think your parents would want you to stop?
- Imagine that your future mate is out there somewhere. You haven't met him yet, but he is in a dating relationship with someone else right now. Where would you want him to stop?
- What would holy and honorable look like?

Think About It

- What do you notice about where all of your lines fell? Were you consistent in where you placed your lines? Why or why not?

- Were there any questions that were hard to answer? If so, why?

- What can you learn about living holy and honorable lives of sexual purity from this exercise?

One season in particular that often is a struggle for couples to stay pure is when they are engaged. These are couples who have set their sights on getting married but aren't to the wedding date yet. Way too often these couples begin to push past boundaries of purity they had previously set. "We are going to get married anyway; it's only natural," they say. Yet if anything, this is a point where sexual purity takes a more prominent place.

You see, it is very important for couples to learn the discipline of purity. If they choose this time to feed their appetite for sex, they are actually choosing to give in to passions rather than controlling them. So after a few months of marriage, when some of the initial excitement of sex begins to settle, where will they go if they have built their relationship on adrenaline? Couples may have thought they were pursuing love but, in reality, were pursing lust. This lack of self-control actually can taint a couple's appetite for genuine, loving sex within the bounds of marriage.

Hard Lessons

Anna and Jeff began dating in high school and continued into college. Halfway through her degree program, Jeff proposed. Thrilled with the thought of spending the rest of their lives together, they began to spend more and more time alone and went further and further into physical intimacy. One month before their wedding date, Jeff was killed in a car accident. Eight months later, Anna gave birth to their son. Engaged does not equal married.

Eric had never kept any real boundaries around his sexual purity with girls he had dated in the past. When he met Alice, she insisted on maintaining purity standards in dating. His response was simply to marry her after only a few months of dating so they could move forward physically. However, just two years into marriage, he confessed to her he had been having an affair with a co-worker. Eric had never really bothered to work at sexual purity. He had just pushed past or around obstacles to satisfy his sexual desires. Without exercising any discipline, he found himself vulnerable to Satan's temptations. Just as physical exercise gives us increased physical strength, exercising our spiritual "muscles" helps us be strong against Satan.

Insights From Bethany

I want to be hungry for God, His righteousness, and everything that falls under those categories (purity, selflessness, patience, etc.). It helps me in the moment of temptation to ask myself, "Would indulging in this thought or action feed my appetite for Christ and His goodness or feed empty lust and selfish desire?" I guess, to me, this is really what "drawing the line" comes down to. If you are training your heart truly to SEEK and DESIRE Christ and His kingdom, you will know, deep down, if your actions and thoughts are bringing you closer to that direction or farther away. Take time to really examine your motives: "Why do I want to do this? Will my actions make my boyfriend/fiance/husband thank Christ for me or cry out to Him for deliverance from sin?" If this love and consideration for your guy and His Creator is not a convincing motivation for you, work so that it is – or break off the relationship. This is really where the rubber meets the road.

Summing It Up

Living a holy and honorable life of sexual purity is one of the ways we accept God's invitation to be with Him and to enjoy the love He offers us. Nothing else compares to choosing this path. By choosing this path, we avoid the confusion that adrenaline and emotion can add to building a relationship (or deciding not to build a relationship) with someone in our lives. This leads to deeper, more lasting relationships that are built on a more secure foundation than the temporary high of physical intimacy.

But choosing this path does involve making clear choices and thinking with our brains in gear before we get in situations where we may be challenged with physical affection. Satan is quite good at taking something God designed for a special purpose and making it evil. In this case, God's design for physical touch and intimacy in marriage is an excellent "glue" to help bond a committed relationship. But glue without the commitment of marriage is just a sticky mess.

Talk About It

1. What are some practical ways women can help one another choose and protect sexual purity?

2. What are some ways dating couples can help each other with this decision?

3. How can a married couple protect their union from being pulled apart by outside influences in this area?

Pray About It

Lord, we want to be where You are, living daily in Your presence. A life without You would be a life of sadness, fear and confusion. Thank You for calling us to You, to a life of holiness that protects us from Satan's lies. Give us wisdom, Lord, to think clearly through the choices we make as Your daughters. May we seek always to please You, our loving Father.

Recommended Reading

• *Every Man's Battle: Winning the War on Sexual Temptation One Victory at a Time* by Stephen Arterburn, Fred Stoeker, and Mike Yorkey (Colorado Springs: WaterBrook, 2009).

• *Every Woman's Battle: Discovering God's Plan for Sexual and Emotional Fulfillment* by Shannon Ethridge (Colorado Springs: Multnomah, 2013).

These two books, one written to men and one to women, explore the battle of maintaining sexual purity. Recognizing the unique challenges that each gender faces, the authors provide specific guidance geared toward these specific battles. I have read them both and found that they both gave insights I needed to guard my life as well as those of the men in my life.

Chapter 13

Loving God Through Purity

Opening Reflections

Balance and gracefulness are not my strong suits. While my husband and I relish a hike through the woods, when we get to a log crossing, I halt. He has to go first to check it out and then usually come back to help me across. I'm afraid of falling because I know I do not have an abundance of natural balance and stability. I need all the help I can get.

Starting Point

Imagine that you want to reach something up high, but the only thing in the room is a table. This is a fairly ordinary table – square in shape, made out of sturdy wood, designed with one strong leg securely attached at each corner. Pretty normal table. Does that sound like something you might use to climb higher? What if one or more of the legs is missing? Would you climb on it then? Why or why not?

In the previous lesson, we saw that God receives our pure sexual life as a gift of love to Him. But while we may want to demonstrate this love to Him, it's not always easy to grasp how that looks on a day-to-day basis. How do I navigate the pressures that would lead me away from loving God through purity? How do I put safety rails around my heart so I don't drift away from my commitment to purity? We will take some time in this lesson to explore some practical ways we can protect our special gift of purity.

 Read About It
  Mark 12:28-31

 Think About It
  • What are the four ways we can demonstrate our love for God?

  • Why do you think Jesus mentioned these four ways specifically? How are they different from one another?

These few short verses tell us a lot about how we can love God in general, but they also provide four important touch points for considering how we can love God through lives of purity. Four areas – our hearts, our souls, our minds and our strength – make up a complete picture of purity. All are needed to be complete. All are important. Let's explore how to embrace purity in these four areas.

Our Hearts

We've already talked about how the hormones related to sexual excitement can lead to feelings of attachment. In the context of marriage, these chemicals are wonderful blessings. However, outside of marriage, they can lead to feelings of attachment that can quickly take the focus off of purity. It makes sense that guarding your heart is an important element in protecting your gift of purity.

How do we protect our hearts? First, staying away from physical touching and kissing that leads to sexual excitement outside of marriage will prevent the release of those hormones, which cause confusion outside of their intended context. So this simply means that you need to find something else to do on your dates besides sitting around hugged up somewhere. That may sound very simplistic, but the reality is that many couples get involved in physical affection because they really didn't have anything else planned to do. Affection is a natural desire that comes from being with someone you care about. So it is easy to just naturally default to touching and kissing. That means you and your date need to do some thinking and planning before you get together.

In general, activities that involve being around other people can help you stay on track toward purity. For instance, going places where you stay out in the public or doing things together with other couples that share your commitment to purity reduces the temptations that threaten the heart. Plan your time together intentionally.

Another way to guard your heart is to seek good friendships. Sometimes when people feel lonely or unloved, they may go "looking for love in all the wrong places" as an old song states. My prayer is that every person reading this has at least one good friend who loves her and with whom she can talk. However, if that is not true for you, one thing I can assure you is that seeking that kind of emotional fulfillment by becoming sexually active will not work. In fact, it will very likely have the opposite effect in the long run.

You see, while a girl might feel some comfort for the moment in the physical affection of a boyfriend, that result won't last. What happens is that when the relationship starts to become focused on the physical (touching, kissing, etc.), efforts to grow the relationship deeper in other areas (emotionally, mentally, spiritually) tend to stop. So while the physical touching may increase, the emotional comfort that comes from having a true friendship actually decreases. This leaves the girl feeling even more lonely and misused.

It just doesn't work. Sex does not equal love, especially for a guy. You remember the hormones? A woman gives a piece of her heart to every person she allows to excite her sexually (touching, lengthy kissing and such). When the guy walks away, he takes that bit of her heart with him.

Read About It

Proverbs 4:23

Think About It

- Why do you think this verse puts so much emphasis on guarding your heart?

- What are some consequences you have seen in those who do not guard their hearts?

- What are some things couples can do to help each other become better friends yet still guard their hearts?

- What are some "heart protectors" that we should put in our lives?

Our Minds

We discussed the importance of thinking clearly about how to control our bodies when we explored 1 Thessalonians 4:1-8 (particularly verse 4). There, God instructed us to "know how to control" our own bodies (ESV). This is one area where we truly have to have our heads in gear to remain pure. As women with all of our emotional connectors going on (spaghetti), losing track of what is important is all too easy if our brains are not clearly focused on the purity plan. So how do we train our brains to guide us through the jungle of sexual lies that Satan has planted in this world?

As with all dangers, the first step is to open your eyes and pay attention. For starters, try this exercise next time you sit down to watch TV. Get out a piece of paper and a pen, and tune your ears and eyes to catch messages about sex. Some of these messages will be stated obviously while others will be more subtle hints of sexual immorality. (Remember the discussion of Ephesians 5?) In a variety of shapes and forms, these messages are everywhere in our culture. Pay attention to characters interacting on TV shows you watch. Are they involved in physical, sexual relationships? What messages do you get from their interactions? What about the commercials? Is cooking rice in the microwave or using the right brand of shampoo really the key for a healthy sexual relationship?

Chances are, when you take time to do this little activity, you will hear and see a lot of things that are against God's plan for healthy sexual intimacy in marriage. You can know for sure that anything that is opposite of what God says comes from Satan. So guarding and training your mind begins by recognizing the enemy and his messages.

If learning to recognize the traps of Satan is step one, step two is refusing to listen. You've heard the phrase "garbage in, garbage out," right? It is certainly true here.

Think About It

When was the last time you turned off the TV or radio or put down a book or magazine because the messages were not in line with God's will?

Maybe for you, that was recently. But I think for many of us getting lulled into tolerating the messages is all too easy, and then we no longer hear them for what they are. Our brains can develop acceptance to

Satan's messages in the same way we can become comfortable with increased physical touch. Remember the frog?

Also, training your brain is not just about avoiding putting junk in; it is also about feeding your brain on spiritually healthy nourishment. From a physical standpoint, we readily recognize that healthy eating is not just avoiding a constant diet of junk food. It also requires us to consume healthy choices like fresh fruits and vegetables and such. So then, what are you feeding your brain?

Read About It
Philippians 4:8

Think About It

- What would it be like to choose all of your TV shows, magazines, movies, music and books through this filter? Would you be making changes from what you are choosing now?

- Why do you think God placed these qualities as guides to what we think?

- How does focusing our brain on these things help us maintain purity?

One final word on the brain before we move on. We women struggle with a temptation for a particular type of brain poison that is as destructive to our purity commitment as pornography is to the guys. This may not be popular, but hear me out. When we are drawn to spending time watching the steamy love stories or curling up on the couch with a passionate romance novel, we are feeding our brains junk food. As women, those kinds of stories appeal to our natural desires for relationships and affection. However, just as pornography sets unrealistic and ungodly pictures before a guy's eyes, these kinds of influences set the same traps in our minds and hearts as women.

These are dangerous to the single woman who is navigating the path of purity and seeking to understand and find a godly mate. But they are just as deadly to those of us who are married because, in either case, they set before us standards and expectations that are not in line with God's will for our lives. Here's the bottom line: Feeding your brain Satan's garbage will lead you to thinking Satan's garbage. And thinking Satan's garbage leads to living it. King Solomon, to whom

God granted a great measure of wisdom, wrote this in Proverbs 23:7: "As [a man] thinks in his heart, so is he" (NKJV).

Insights From Bethany

Root yourself in reality. It often helps, when holding up our thoughts to the filter of Philippians 4:8, to focus on the very first one: "whatever things are true" (NKJV). Anything that falls under the category of "wouldn't it be nice if ..." or "if I could just be her for a day with someone like him ... " is based in a fairy-tale reality. "If" is fiction. Does it make much sense to base the yearnings of our hearts on something (or someone) that is fictitious?

Instead, I train my mind to think of real Christian couples and parents that I know. What do their stories look like? Does their kind of love match up with what I'm seeing on TV or reading? Talking to faithful Christian couples is so much more reliable than any author or movie director who will often sacrifice truth for feel-good sensations and true depictions of love for sexual excitement (and who have no obligation to present the world according to reality).

An Example

Rebecca was an avid reader throughout high school. She would polish off a cheap romance book almost once a day. Part of the reason she could read these so quickly was because she learned how to skim to the "good parts" – the steamy romance scenes. Rocking on through her college years, she continued to read these stories, reinforcing these scenes in her mind again and again. So as you might imagine, when she entered into marriage, she had some deeply ingrained expectations. Then, reality set in. Her godly husband, loving as he was, did not always do or say just the right things to sweep her off her feet. Sometimes he was insensitive, distracted or just plain rude – just as we all are as humans.

However, her four-plus years of engraving false expectations into her brain created real problems in accepting her mate, flaws and all. It was not until several years into her marriage, after she confessed her "book affair" to her husband and ceased reading this material, that she began to align her brain toward a pure respect, appreciation and love for her husband. The turning was painful and tough. The "good parts" of books have the ability to foster the release of the sexual excitement hormones. These create cravings that are similar to addictions.

Completely removing that source was not an easy task. Rebecca often expresses how she wished she'd never gotten hooked on those books.

Think About It

What are some specific expectations that a woman might get from romantic fiction that could hinder her walk as a single woman? as a married woman?

Our Strength

While physical strength is certainly a part of this, I believe it also involves our resolve. Have you ever "set your heels" against doing something? Someone tried to get you to do something (good or bad), and you crossed your arms, set your heels, and essentially said, "No, and you can't make me!" You were determined, and you were ready for battle if that is what it took to stand your ground.

This, I believe, is a good picture of what it means to use your strength to love God through purity. You are ready to do battle against Satan to protect yourself and those around you. It is a **strength** that comes from setting your **mind** to guard your **heart**. (Notice how those three elements work together.) Without this resolve, you will be unprepared to use your strength to protect your purity.

So let's say you are ready to use your strength for purity. How would that look? Let's explore one way. In the '80s and '90s, the "Just Say No" campaign started being promoted throughout the U.S. It was a message to stand up against anyone trying to push you to drugs and simply say no. A loud and clear message. No misunderstandings or wishy-washy answers – just a clear "No!" Kids practiced saying no in drug education programs, and commercials aired frequently on TV with kids modeling the message.

Although that was targeted to drug prevention, some clear guidelines were there that work well against any temptation. First, giving a clear, unmuddled message of where you stand is essential. If someone is tempting you to step outside the boundaries of purity, your first response is to clearly tell him no. And don't give him one of those "well I, um, probably shouldn't do this 'cause, um, I might get in trouble or something" kinds of responses. Stand up. Be strong. Be clear. And say no. You don't have to offer any kind of long explanation or make any excuses. Just say no.

If someone continues to pressure you after you have said a clear no, you may want to consider his motives. Remember that if someone is seeking something out of selfishness, it is not love. So if someone is trying to get you to do something that you know is wrong, chances are he is acting out of selfishness. That should be a major red flag to you. Pay attention!

But let's say that he continues to pressure you. Your second line of defense is to turn that challenge around. Ask him in clear words, "Why do you keep pressuring me to do something that I do not want to do?" A true friend will listen and honor the challenge. But if this does not stop the pressure, get up and get out – immediately! Don't play around with this kind of pressure. If it means calling your folks or a trusted friend to come get you, do it. If it means walking out of the room to join a different group of friends, start walking. Whatever it takes to get out of the situation, do it.

One very important guideline here is this: Don't put yourself in a situation where you can't leave safely. For instance, sitting with your boyfriend in his car on a deserted road is not a place you can leave safely. Don't get yourself in that kind of situation. This is not a game. There is too much at stake for you to play around with your physical or spiritual safety. Use your strength to protect your purity.

 ## Read About It
Ephesians 6:10-11

 ## Think About It

- What pictures does the idea of putting on armor bring to your mind? What sort of setting do you see? Why is the armor important in that setting?

- Where does our power come from according to these verses? How does it feel to have that source available to you?

Our Souls

As we have discussed all through these chapters, our relationship with God is at the core of everything. He loves us and wants to protect us as His beloved children. As we come to understand and accept His offer of love, our natural response is to love Him back. We have seen in our previous studies how He sees our purity as a gift of love to

Him, and the really cool thing about all of that is that our gift of purity to Him ultimately becomes a gift that we receive back. As we follow God's plan of purity, we are the ones who truly gain in the process. (Our loving Father knew that! Isn't He amazing?) So following His guidance is a gift of love to Him because it demonstrates our trust in Him as our loving, protective Father.

So how do we strengthen this avenue of our purity?

Read About It
James 4:7-8

Think About It
- Three steps are given in these verses from James: (1) submit to God, (2) resist the devil, and (3) draw near to God. Why do you think these three steps are important?

- How does it make you feel to picture God drawing nearer to you as you move nearer to Him?

- What are some practical ways we can move closer to God to help strengthen our gift of purity in this area?

Read About It
2 Timothy 2:22

Think About It
Paul told the young Timothy to "flee youthful lusts and pursue righteousness, faith, love and peace." Why do you think he said both to flee lusts and to pursue these other things?

The contrast in this verse clearly reminds us that this battle is far from passive. We have two active charges here. The first one: Flee youthful lusts. Get out of there – now! Flee is a very active word. But we weren't only told to flee. It takes more than simply not sinning to protect our souls. So in this verse, Paul also told us to replace sin with something better, actively seeking to obey God out of love. Our second charge is to pursue righteousness, faith, love and peace. This is not passive either. "Pursue" is an active verb requiring lots of energy.

So next time you are considering a direction to take in a situation, ask yourself what actions would demonstrate fleeing Satan and what actions would demonstrate pursuing God. If you can honestly answer those questions, you will have a clear picture of which way to head as you seek to love God with all your soul in your gift of purity.

Summing It Up

As with all that God does for us, His gift of loving guidance leads us to a life of purity as well as to a life that escapes some of the many hurts that Satan would love to inflict on us through his evil traps. So as we demonstrate our love to God for His care, we engage our minds, hearts, strength and souls in the process. But the amazing thing about God's love is that while we are demonstrating our love to Him, we are ultimately the ones who benefit. We cannot out-love God. He is our amazing Father!

 ## Talk About It

1. How does considering purity from all four of these avenues strengthen a person's resolve to live a pure life?

2. What would happen if one of them was missing?

3. How can we, as women, encourage one another in each of these areas?

4. How can we protect and encourage the guys in our lives in each area?

Pray About It

Our precious Father, how can we ever even begin to thank You enough for the many, many ways You demonstrate Your love to us daily? We are constantly amazed at the countless expressions of Your love and protection of us as Your dear children. Help us to accept Your love fully and, in trusting faith, respond with hearts, minds, bodies and souls deeply loving You.

Recommended Reading

Following are some Christian fiction novels that do not go into the realm of sensual romance. However, even among Christian novels, some love stories can set unrealistic expectations for Christian marriages. Choose wisely. Just because it says "Christian" on the cover does not mean it will help you gain realistic expectations.

• ***The Centurion's Wife*** by Davis Bunn and Janette Oke (Blooming-ton: Bethany House, 2009). This fictional story surrounds a centurion and his wife set in the days following Jesus' crucifixion. The centurion, as the story is told, was in charge of the events of Jesus' death yet seeks to learn the truth. (Disclaimer: Near the end, the command of Acts 2:38 is mentioned, but it seems to be ignored in practice.)

• ***Mark of the Lion: A Voice in the Wind, An Echo in the Darkness, As Sure as the Dawn*** by Francine Rivers (Wheaton: Tyndale House, 1998). Being a Christian in the days of Roman persecution was challenging at best and, at times, deadly. Living that commitment as a slave in a Roman household added even more challenges.

• ***The Robe*** by Lloyd C. Douglas (New York: Mariner Books, 1999). Although this book has been around since before my time and yours, I just recently discovered it. It is a powerful story set in the context of the time period immediately following Jesus' death.

Supplemental Thoughts

While this book is primarily written to single women, the subject of purity applies to all woman – single, married, divorced or widowed. So if you are not single, here are brief explanations of how purity might apply to you:

• **Married women.** If we are married, then it may be easy to brush this discussion off by saying: "Yeah, yeah. Been there, done that. My wedding day is over. Now it's just down to 'real life' day-to-day stuff."

Yet keeping your marriage a priority is more important now than it was to keep your future spouse a priority. You see, now you have coupled the original interest you had in him to a commitment that is God-sealed. So maintaining your pure commitment to your husband is an essential element of your gift of purity to God.

It is so easy to let time erase from our minds the pledge we took to our husbands to love and honor them above all others. Moving from dating to day-to-day oneness with another person means that you know the other person much more completely than you did when you were just dating. You know the very best about him … and the very worst. It is so easy to settle your focus on the worst or just neglect to think at all. Your gift of purity, then, takes shape in how you think about your husband, how you respond to him, and how you choose him above all others – warts and all.

• **Divorced women.** For those who have experienced divorce, you could no doubt tell us all of the heartache that comes from broken promises and shattered commitments. Regardless of the circumstances that brought you to this place in your life, I am certain you have experienced a pain that few of us can comprehend. So what is the point of purity now? Who cares?

There are several really good answers to that, starting with yourself. You see, in addition to purity being your gift to God, as we have discussed, it is also a gift you give yourself. Although your decision of purity now cannot undo whatever has already happened, it can place you on a solid path that can prevent a world of future hurts and disappointments that would serve only to beat you down physically and emotionally.

• **Widowed women.** And to those who have lost their spouses to death. It is so hard to face the aching emptiness that exists when your one-flesh partner is gone. The pain of having half of you ripped away can seem almost unbearable at times. The hunger in your soul leads some women to seek out the comfort of another man, even to the point of compromising sexual purity. Although this may seem like an easy fix to a broken heart, it only serves to drive even more nails into your shattered heart.

Chapter 14

Is It True Love?

Opening Reflections

I had a friend in college who was "in love" with someone new on what seemed like a daily basis. At one point, she was "in love" with a guy from her hometown. Then she met another guy while traveling and fell "in love" and moved to yet another town, where she instantly fell "in love" with a third guy. She had declared her love and interest in marrying each of these three because she was "sure" they were the right ones … until she met the next one. All of this happened within the space of only a few weeks. Do you know anyone like this?

Starting Point

Early in our series of studies together, we talked about the many kinds of love described in the Bible. Our world is so confused by the concept of love. Part of that confusion comes from the role that emotion plays in the process. It is easy to mistake feelings of excitement we get when we are with someone we like or find attractive for the deep, long-term roots of true love. But while it is difficult to separate the two, recognizing the difference is vital.

You see, our emotions come and go based on circumstances, such as physical health, our stress level, how tired we feel, or even the weather.

With so many things affecting our emotions, sometimes these emotions lead us off in the wrong direction – both away from what we need to do and toward what we do not need to do. More specifically, our emotions can lead us to feel "in love" or "out of love" based on things that are not good measures of true love.

Given all of this, I'm not surprised when I hear someone ask, "How will I know it is true love?" We all know couples who thought they shared true love – and maybe they did – but something happened that landed them in divorce court. Were these couples wrong in identifying true love? Or did they just lose it along the way?

The truth is, probably both reasons are true for some couples. So how can we, as women – married or single – navigate through these confusing waters? Is it all just a big guessing game, or is there something we can really identify as a good measuring stick for true love?

Thanks be to God! He knew we would need some help with this and provided answers.

 Read About It

1 Corinthians 13:4-8

 Think About It

How does this description of love differ from what the world show-cases as love?

An Example

Amy found an interesting use of this passage. Tom had just recently become a Christian and was excited about his new relationship with the Lord. Within a week of his new commitment, he met Amy, who was also a Christian. The next week, the two went on their first date – just getting acquainted. However, on date number three, just a couple of weeks later, Tom got down on one knee and proposed to Amy.

She was very surprised, as you might imagine. She hardly knew this guy, and he certainly didn't know her. How can you know you love someone when you don't even know the person? So she brought him into the kitchen and opened her Bible to this passage, and they read it together. She told him that when they both were to the point of demonstrating these qualities toward each other consistently, then they could start considering marriage.

Did it work? Well, about a year and a half later, they married and are still happily married having raised two boys to adulthood. So maybe there is something to this definition. Let's take a more detailed look at what is there.

These few short verses offer 16 different descriptions of love. Because we may not all be reading from the same version, provided below is a list of what three versions say in these verses. By looking at all three, we can get a pretty good picture of what love is.

ESV	NASB	NKJV
• Patient	• Patient	• Suffers long
• Kind	• Kind	• Kind
• Does not envy	• Not jealous	• Does not envy
• Does not boast	• Does not brag	• Does not parade itself
• Is not arrogant	• Is not arrogant	• Is not puffed up
• Is not rude	• Does not act unbecomingly	• Does not behave rudely
• Does not insist on its own way	• Does not seek its own	• Does not seek its own
• Is not irritable	• Is not provoked	• Is not provoked
• Is not resentful	• Does not take into account a wrong suffered	• Thinks no evil
• Does not rejoice at wrongdoing	• Does not rejoice in unrighteousness	• Does not rejoice in iniquity
• Rejoices with the truth	• Rejoices with the truth	• Rejoices in the truth
• Bears all things	• Bears all things	• Bears all things
• Believes all things	• Believes all things	• Believes all things
• Hopes all things	• Hopes all things	• Hopes all things
• Endures all things	• Endures all things	• Endures all things
• Never ends	• Never fails	• Never fails

Some of these traits we probably all understand pretty well, but some are a little more challenging to grasp. Let's take a few minutes to make sure we understand what God was saying to us. To make this easier, we are going to follow two characters. One is named Love because this is the person who will be acting out love's traits. The other person is Joy because that is what it feels like to be truly loved.

Let's start at the top. Being **patient** or longsuffering with someone means that Love isn't quick to get angry or write Joy off when she messes up or doesn't get something done quite as quickly or quite in the way that Love thought it should be done. Love keeps his cool while helping Joy learn a new skill. Or sometimes it isn't about Joy learning something new. It may be that Joy just does something in a different way from Love. But Love is patient with the difference, even if it is not the way he would do it.

Love is **kind** when he considers the words he says to and about Joy. He is careful not to put her down or purposely hurt her with his words or actions. He is considerate. He seeks to demonstrate kindness to her in every way he can.

Love is **not jealous** of Joy. When she accomplishes something, he is happy with and for her. Love doesn't pout when Joy wins the Monopoly game. Love doesn't mope and grumble when Joy makes a better grade on a test or gets a raise or a promotion that he didn't get. Instead, Love celebrates with Joy.

Now, all of us have things we do better than someone else. God gave each of us strengths to help us through life. However, Love **does not brag** or boast about his strengths. Instead, he gently offers his help when he can out of kindness. Love would never want to make Joy feel inferior or less important by bragging about himself. So if Love is the one with the better grade and Joy is the one feeling sad about her "F," Love would say: "Hey, Joy, you can get this. Let's spend time studying together this week. I'll help you with the places that are hard. I know you can do it."

Closely related to not bragging, Love is **not arrogant**. Arrogance comes from a heart that is proud and considers itself superior to someone else. Love would never place himself above Joy, but instead recognizes each of their strengths as complements in their relationship.

An interesting trait of Love is encompassed in the phrase **"does not act unbecomingly"** or "is not rude." The original Greek carries the idea of acting in accordance to form or shape. Thinking back to how we are formed or shaped, Love acts in keeping with how God designed him and Joy. This leads to not being rude or inappropriate in any way. Instead, Love is honoring and respectful of Joy.

Love is **not self-seeking**, does not seek his own wants above those of Joy. Instead, Love considers Joy's wants and needs in the decisions he makes. That doesn't mean that Love never does anything that he wants, but rather that he does not run over Joy or her feelings while he pursues things that he may want or need. For instance, suppose Love is a husband who enjoys golfing. He has found a new set of clubs that he'd like to have. But when he sits down with Joy to look at the family budget and needs of the family, he realizes that the family needs will take all of the available money this month. He chooses to wait for the clubs so that he can care for his family first.

Love is **not easily angered.** Now, that doesn't mean that he will never become angry, but notice that he will not be *easily* angered. That means he doesn't fly off the handle every time something doesn't go just right. It takes a lot for Love to become angry. And when he does become angry, he still demonstrates love. So when Love becomes angry, he is still kind. He does not strike out with his words or with his hands. Love does not hit in anger. (Girls, if your guy hits you once, chances are he will hit you again if he does not get help.) He is careful of what he says so that he does not hurt Joy out of anger.

Love **does not keep a record of wrongs**. You have probably heard someone say something like, "That's the third time this week you have done that." That's what it means to keep a record of wrongs. You see, when Love forgives a wrong that Joy has done, he forgets it. He doesn't keep bringing it back up to her once it is forgiven. Imagine what it would be like if God kept a record of all of our wrongs. That would be an overwhelming burden. The same is true in a close human relationship.

If you are with someone for a long time, your list of mistakes will be long, as will the other person's. It is important for Love to deal with those hurts when they happen, but once forgiveness has taken place, he must let them go. Where this may get confusing is when there is a destructive behavior involved. Suppose that a guy hits his girl when he is angry. Or maybe he abuses alcohol or drugs as a way of getting through life. These kinds of ongoing destructive behaviors need attention. Loving him would mean that she works to get him the help he needs to deal with these behaviors.

The next two traits of love go together. Love **does not rejoice in evil** but **rejoices in the truth**. You probably know people who love to dig up dirt on others and spread it around. It usually doesn't matter a whole lot to those people exactly how true what they are spreading is. Love takes an opposite approach. First, Love checks the facts and does not go off on half-truths and gossip. Second, even if a wrong has been done, Love would never spread the information to others. Gossip and hurtful rumors are the opposite of Love. How Love talks about Joy to other people is included here. Love would never tell hurtful stories about Joy to his friends just to get a laugh.

You see, by demonstrating these traits, Love will always seek to protect Joy. He does not want to see her hurt by others or himself. He is considerate and watchful to ensure that she feels safe.

Love **always trusts**. I have known people who are quick to assume the worst about someone else. But Love trusts Joy. I can remember early in my own marriage that my husband and I would often get into quarrels that were really about one of us thinking the other had been inconsiderate. It was a huge turning point in our relationship when we decided to always trust each other to be acting out of love. How that looks in real terms is this: When he is late coming home and hasn't called, instead of assuming he doesn't care or is being inconsiderate, I wonder if he may have had car trouble or perhaps had an opportunity to visit with someone who needed to talk. I may call to make sure he is okay, but I'm not already angry because I have assumed the worst. Instead, I'm eager to hear his voice and learn of opportunities he may have had.

Love **always hopes** and **perseveres**. Both of these traits have an eye to the future. Both mean that Love is in it for the long haul, ready to go the distance. Love is ready to move with Joy into the future. So he is hopeful and encouraging as he looks forward. And even when hard times hit, Love perseveres or stays steady. Love is not wishy-washy in his relationship with Joy. Love treats Joy with love through good times and bad, for better or worse, in sickness and in health, for richer or poorer. Sound familiar? Love stays the course.

Love **never fails**. Now that is a pretty tall order for us humans, and the reality is none of us can completely live up to this. However, Love – although he is human – will be consistent in his actions toward Joy. Not sinlessly perfect, but consistently loving. And when he does make a mistake, he will be quick to seek forgiveness from Joy and get back on track.

Think About It

Which of these traits in your opinion are easiest to spot in another person? Which ones are hardest to spot? What makes the difference?

So how do I know if it is true love? The answer is based on God's description of love in 1 Corinthians 13. But here's what you have to realize: You cannot truly know if your guy is going to demonstrate these characteristics toward you over the long haul until you have seen him hold this course for a long time. That means you need to see how he will act over time, in lots of different circumstances, and through lots of different emotions.

You see, as humans, most of us can be on our best behavior for a short time no matter what. So even guys who are self-seeking might be able to act loving for a short time so they can get what they want. But time tells the truth. If a guy can consistently hold these traits over a long period of time, then he may be the real thing. Not many of us can fake it for a long time.

Now, let's turn the tables because a truly long-term loving relationship is built between two people. So suppose you find this great guy who loves you dearly. What does your side of the relationship look like?

Think About It

Look back at the lists on page 145. Which characteristics are easy for you to demonstrate? Which ones are harder?

Read About It
• Mark 12:28-31
• John 13:35
• 1 John 4:19-21

You see, in these passages Jesus called us to demonstrate this kind of love toward everyone. This is not something we can just turn off or on at will when we find someone who treats us right. These are traits that God expects of His children as His hands, His feet and His voice in this world.

Summing It Up

So this chapter is really two parts:

Part 1: How do I know if someone really loves me? Look at his behavior. Does it match the description of love in 1 Corinthians 13? If not, then your answer is no. And if that's the case, rethink that relationship. Although you may choose to be friends with lots of people, you do not want to marry someone who does not demonstrate love for you.

Part 2: How am I doing in demonstrating love to the people around me? And that includes everyone – not just the guy you are interested in at the moment or your best friend. You see, if you are just acting loving toward someone in whom you are interested or toward someone who is treating you with love, then you are self-seeking. That's not love. Love is consistent, no matter what.

 Talk About It

1. What are some specific characteristics of love you see in God or in His Son, Jesus?

2. What is one specific change you can make this week to become more loving toward those around you?

Pray About It

Our precious Father, thank You for such a clear picture of love. Help us to demonstrate this love in our lives daily. Lord, please guide those who are not married to examine carefully their potential mates through this lens so they can discern relationships that are built in love. Help us to have strong families that honor You.

Recommended Reading

Love Is a Decision: Proven Techniques to Keep Your Marriage Alive and Lively by Gary Smalley and John Trent (Nashville: Thomas Nelson, 2001). Authors Smalley and Trent provide practical guidance in applying *agape* love in a marriage relationship. The decision to treat each other with love fosters a marriage to go the distance.

Chapter 15

The Celebration

Opening Reflections

Ask any married woman about her wedding day, and you will likely find that she can recall the event in great detail regardless of how many years have passed. She will probably be able to describe her dress, preparations for the ceremony, the participants in the wedding party, and details of the actual ceremony – along with one or two funny things that happened along the way. You will also hear her tell of the emotions of the day. For many married women, this is one of the most significant days of their lives.

Starting Point

From the time we were little girls, many of us dreamed of being someone's beautiful bride. We watched *Cinderella*, *Sleeping Beauty* and *Snow White* with wonder as Prince Charming came to claim his lovely bride. It was a wonderful celebration!

As a young bride-to-be, a girl often starts poring over magazines looking for the perfect dress, the perfect hairstyle, and just the right flowers to accent her perfect day. She wants to look her best for that special moment when she enters the room to present herself to her husband.

That precious moment signals the beginning of a unique, unmatchable union that is to last and grow for the rest of her life!

Think About It

- What would you think of a bride who put absolutely no thought into how she looked on her wedding day?

- How do you think the groom would feel if she just forgot to show up? ("Oh, was that today? I'm sorry. I got distracted with this TV show.")

Can you imagine the disappointment a groom might feel if the bride just absolutely neglected to prepare for the wedding day? Or worse, forgot to show up? What are the chances they would even get married at that point? I figure that, at least, the groom would want to step back and reexamine his decision. But I also imagine that if she continued to show a lack of consideration or concern for the relationship, he would probably bow out of the engagement and walk away.

Yet there is a level of preparation to a wedding that runs so much deeper than just the bride's outward beauty. Imagine now that this same woman engaged to this same wonderful guy takes a different approach to their wedding day. Oh, she is eagerly shopping for the perfect dress, hairstyle and flowers. She invests all of her time, energy and money so she can be sure to look just right. But in the process, she neglects the relationship with her husband-to-be and even goes so far as to cheat on him with an old boyfriend whom she decided she needed to see just one last time – only that one last time turned into a one-night fling.

So here she is now, making her grand entrance into the chapel to meet her groom, and she looks fabulous! As she makes her way down the aisle, everyone beams with delight. Excited whispers move through the crowd: "Isn't she beautiful?" But no one is as enthralled as the groom. His eyes widen with amazement as this gorgeous woman makes her way to his side. His heart is about to burst with joy!

But you know what has happened. He doesn't. Well, at least not until the preacher gets to the part where he says, "If anyone knows a reason that these two should not marry, let him speak now or forever hold his peace." In walks the man with whom she cheated. He shares what she has done – how she has defiled and betrayed her loyal fiance.

Think About It

- How would the groom feel at this point? How do you think he would react?

- Which would be worse: not taking time to prepare outwardly (dress, hair, etc.) or not taking time to prepare inwardly (protecting the relationship)? Why?

While most of us would probably say that the cheating, broken relationship was the deeper hurt, both active betrayal and purposeful neglect are relationship poison. Both reflect a condition of the heart and are very real examples of how we may choose to respond to Jesus as our Bridegroom – but we'll get to that in a second.

An ideal picture, then, of a loving bride would be described in different terms. We would see her carefully preparing on her wedding day, eager to present herself adorned in radiant clothing – spotless and beautiful. But her wedding day preparation would not have started just in the few hours, days or even weeks before her moment to walk down the aisle. Instead, her preparation would have been a heart preparation as she protected herself in purity, waiting for the moment when she could walk forward to present herself to him alone. Ultimately, it is the heart of the relationship that will set the course over time.

So what about you? Maybe you are thinking you would like to be married someday, or maybe you are even engaged. Few things will challenge a marriage more than going into it with a trail of consequences from a life lived outside of purity. The more you have played around with sexual immorality, the harder it will be for you to commit in marriage.

Does that mean you are doomed to divorce if you have been involved in sex before marriage? No, but the reality is you will face some challenges that those who have remained sexually pure until marriage will not face. So for those who have steered clear of sexual immorality so far, stay on that course. You will be tempted to veer off, but if you do marry later on, you will discover that staying on the path of purity was worth the work.

You see, no matter who we are or where we are, the path that God places before us leads us to the greatest joy we can attain. Here is what is so exciting: There is a great mystery carefully woven into the life of purity, a mystery that is so amazing that it is hard to put into words.

Read About It

- Revelation 19:7-8
- Ephesians 5:25-32

Think About It

- Who is the bride in these verses? Who is the bridegroom?

- How does it make you feel to think of being the bride of Christ?

- What evidence do you see that the bride prepared herself for the wedding day?

- How does Christ prepare us for that day?

Does it not just completely blow you away to think about being the bride of Christ? Sharing the love and the day-to-day oneness with our Lord and Savior is just more than I can imagine! Yet until you have accepted the seat of honor offered by our Lord to be His bride, you cannot wholly prepare to be the bride of any human.

Here's why: As humans, we will continually blow it. No matter how perfect we want to be in our love for one another, we will make mistakes out of ignorance, weariness or selfishness. Humans are like that. So when one human marries another human, guess what? You have twice the mistakes and twice the opportunities to fail.

So how does Christ change that? For starters, He alone demonstrates a pure and spotless love. It is in allowing Him into our lives that we begin to mirror His love. It is this kind of love that we saw described in 1 Corinthians 13. Reading that description, you may have thought: "Whew! I'm a long way from having this all figured out." Yet Christ in us can help us learn how to show that kind of love daily. Then, our actions become dependent upon Him, not dependent upon our mate's actions.

In any marriage there will be times that challenge even the best of relationships. A commitment to Christ, first and foremost, can help sustain a marriage even when nothing else is going right. There have been times in our marriage when we have been so low that every day was a challenge to navigate. During some of those times, it would have seemed the easy way out to just walk away and start over somewhere else. But I remembered that at the exact moment that I made a commitment to my husband to be faithful to him until death parts us, I also made a commitment to my Lord to hold my marriage vow. So even if I have a moment when I'm not thrilled to be married to my husband, I know that my commitment to my Lord rises far above how I may be feeling at the moment toward my spouse.

Regardless of who you are and where you are, here is an absolute truth: No human can completely fulfill you. If you are without Christ in your life, you will always feel a void. No matter who he is or how wonderful he is, no human male can take Jesus' place in your life. Your guy may be a nice guy. He may even be a great guy. But he is still a human guy with human weaknesses.

And you? You are still a human woman. That means that no matter how well-meaning you may be, you are going to blow it. You cannot be the be-all and end-all for any man, no matter how much you want to be. And no guy can be that for you either. You need Jesus. Your guy needs Jesus. You are not fully prepared to be someone else's bride until you have given yourself to Christ as His bride – prepared and adorned, ready to be His first, above all else.

My Story

I didn't date much in high school because I was very serious about dating a Christian and there just weren't many guys in our small congregation. So I waited until I went to Freed-Hardeman University, a Christian college, to begin dating with any real seriousness. At that time (and maybe even still today), there was a joke that a girl went to Freed to get her "MRS" degree or, in other words, to find a mate. Although it was intended as a joke, the reality was many women found Christian mates while pursuing their degrees. But that just didn't seem to be working out for me.

Although I had dated several great Christian guys during my four years of college, I had not found one with whom I wanted to spend the rest of my life. As I began my senior year, I felt a little panicky. I began to look around trying to figure out whom I was going to marry before it was too late (defined in my mind by graduation). I pursued and dated with this same sense of urgency. I've got to find a mate – and quickly!

As you can imagine, this approach led to a lot of frustration and hurt, both on my part as well as on the part of some godly young men.

During my very last semester, though, as I was doing my student teaching practicum, God grabbed my heart. When I wasn't in the classroom or preparing lessons, I began to run, partly as a way of burning off my frustration. During those long daily runs, I began to pray to God. My prayers started out being expressions of frustration: "What's wrong with me, Lord, that no one wants me?" and "Why can't I find someone? I've been waiting my whole life for a godly mate? Why can't I have one?"

During the following weeks, God began gently to move in my heart as our daily talks continued. My prayers became "Lord, Your will be done. I will wait on Your timing." Then, I moved one more step closer to Him: "Lord, I will be content being Your bride, regardless of whatever else does or doesn't happen in my life." The moment I voiced that commitment to Him for the first time, I felt a sense of peace like never before – a peace that passes understanding, as God had promised (Philippians 4:6-7). Clearly, that was where I needed to be. The next few weeks, as I closed out my final semester at college, brought a tremendous sense of peace and comfort. My heart had shifted from trying to fill a void with a human to looking to God to complete me.

God has a plan. Although it may not mean marriage for each of us, He is faithful in holding us securely and lovingly when we place Him as our first and foremost Bridegroom. I am convinced that we cannot be a suitable bride for a man until we have completely given ourselves over to being the bride of Christ.

Summing It Up

We are invited to a celebration – one in which Jesus comes for His bride, the church. His bride waits eagerly for Him to return – dressed in white, pure and ready. As a part of His church, His bride, we can prepare for that wedding day celebration, and as we prepare for the day when He will come back to claim us, we are better prepared for experiencing human relationships here. Without our Lord in our lives, whether we are single or married, we will find many, many more challenges pulling and tugging us away from purity. Strive to be the bride of Christ!

Talk About It

1. How does the imagery of Christ's wedding day make you feel?

2. How does preparing to be Christ's bride help a woman prepare for an earthly marriage?

3. What challenges will a couple face when they do not have Christ in their lives?

Pray About It

Jesus, our precious Bridegroom, help us prepare for our wedding day. We want to be ready. We eagerly wait for You to come and claim us. As we wait, help us to keep our eyes set toward that day and keep our lives clean and adorned in white so we are ready to meet You. Lord, help our devotion to You to impact the relationships that surround us. Help us to treat those around us with the love You would choose to show. God, bless our homes and marriages – the ones that exist now and the ones that will be in our futures. We wait eagerly for our wedding day!

Endnotes

Chapter 2

1 "Wonderfully (*palah*)," Strong's Exhaustive Concordance of the Bible (1890): n.pag., *SwordSearcher*, CD-ROM (Broken Arrow: StudyLamp Software, 1995–2012).

2 "Fearfully (*yare*)" Strong's.

Chapter 3

1 Henry George Liddell and Robert Scott, "Love (*eros*)," A Greek-English Lexicon (Oxford: Clarendon Press, 1940).

2 "Love (*phileo*)" Strong's.

3 "Love (*storge*)" Strong's.

4 "Love (*agape*)" Strong's.

Chapter 4

1 "Help (*ezer*)" Strong's.

2 "Meet (*neged*)" Strong's.

Chapter 5

1 "Fornication (*porneia*)" Strong's.

2 "Adultery (*moichao*)" Strong's.

Chapter 7

1 Significant volumes of research have sought to define human emotional needs. Although not completely without criticism, Maslow's hierarchy of needs defines a set of emotional needs fairly common to mankind. Within the context of marriage literature, these emotional needs are often explored more deeply as they relate to specific gender roles and brain design. As noted in the text of this book, the six identified needs tend to be top emotional needs, and the tendency is for males and females to relate to them differently.

Chapter 8

1 Joe S. McIlhaney and Freda McKissic Bush, *Hooked: New Science on How Casual Sex Is Affecting Our Children* (Chicago: Northfield Pub., 2008). This book supplied the information about oxytocin and vasopressin in this chapter.

Chapter 9

1 Centers for Disease Control and Prevention, *Sexually Transmitted Disease Surveillance 2010* (Atlanta: U.S. Department of Health and Human Services, 2011), 10 Nov. 2012 <http://www.cdc.gov/std/stats10/exordium.htm>.

2 Medical Institute for Sexual Health, "How many STIs are there and what are their names?", 17 Apr. 2013 <https://www.medinstitute.org/resources/faqs>.

3 Centers for Disease Control and Prevention, "Pelvic Inflammatory Disease (PID) CDC Fact Sheet," 10 Nov. 2012 <http://www.cdc.gov/std/PID/STDFact-PID.htm>.

4 Centers for Disease Control and Prevention, "Syphilis CDC Fact Sheet," 10 Nov. 2012 <http://www.cdc.gov/std/syphilis/STDFact-Syphilis.htm>.

5 Centers for Disease Control and Prevention, "Hepatitis Information for the Public," 17 Apr. 2013 <www.cdc.gov/hepatitis/PublicInfo.htm>.

6 Centers for Disease Control and Prevention, "Genital Herpes CDC Fact Sheet," 10 Nov. 2012 <http://www.cdc.gov/std/herpes/STDFact-Herpes.htm>.

7 Centers for Disease Control and Prevention, "The Role of STD Detection and Treatment in HIV Prevention CDC Fact Sheet," 10 Nov. 2012 <http://www.cdc.gov/std/hiv/STDFact-STD-HIV.htm>.

8 Centers for Disease Control and Prevention, "Genital HPV Infection Fact Sheet," 10 Nov. 2012 <http://www.cdc.gov/std/HPV/STDFact-HPV.htm>.

9 U.S. Department of Health and Human Services Office on Women's Health, "Birth Control Methods Fact Sheet," 18 Apr. 2013 <www.womenshealth.gov/publications/our-publications/fact-sheet/birth-control-methods.cfm#d>.

Chapter 10

1 C.P. Cowan and P.A. Cowan, "Who Does What When Partners Become Parents: Implications for Men, Women, and Marriage," *Transitions to Parenthood*, eds. R. Palkovitz and M.B. Sussman (New York: The Haworth Press, 1988) 105-131.

2 Xi-Kuan Chen, Shi Wu Wen, N. Fleming, K. Demissie, G. Rhoads, and M. Walker, "Teenage Pregnancy and Adverse Birth Outcomes: A Large Population Based Retrospective Cohort Study," *International Journal of Epidemiology*. 36.2(2007): 368-73.

3 National Poverty Center, "Poverty in the United States," 10 Nov. 2012. <http://www.npc.umich.edu/poverty/>.

Leader's Guide

Also available from the Gospel Advocate, *The Gift of Purity – Leader's Guide*. To see a sample from this guide – which has explanations, suggestions and notes from the author as well as extra activities for groups studies of *The Gift of Purity* – visit the Gospel Advocate website at www.gospeladvocate.com. To purchase, follow the instructions on the website, and download the leader's guide to your computer or tablet.

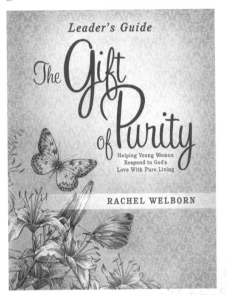

Leader's Guide

The **Gift** *of* **Purity**

Helping Young Women
Respond to God's
Love With Pure Living

RACHEL WELBORN

G56358 $4.99

Visit us on Facebook

www.facebook.com/giftofpurity